Georgia Geometry EOC

SUCCESS STRATEGIES

**Georgia EOC Test Review
for the Georgia End of
Course Tests**

Need more help? Check out our flashcards at: http://MometrixFlashcards.com/Georgia

TABLE OF CONTENTS

Top 15 Test Taking Tips

1. Know the test directions, duration, topics, question types, how many questions
2. Setup a flexible study schedule at least 3-4 weeks before test day
3. Study during the time of day you are most alert, relaxed, and stress free
4. Maximize your learning style; visual learner use visual study aids, auditory learner use auditory study aids
5. Focus on your weakest knowledge base
6. Find a study partner to review with and help clarify questions
7. Practice, practice, practice
8. Get a good night's sleep; don't try to cram the night before the test
9. Eat a well balanced meal
10. Wear comfortable, loose fitting, layered clothing; prepare for it to be either cold or hot during the test
11. Eliminate the obviously wrong answer choices, then guess the first remaining choice
12. Pace yourself; don't rush, but keep working and move on if you get stuck
13. Maintain a positive attitude even if the test is going poorly
14. Keep your first answer unless you are positive it is wrong
15. Check your work, don't make a careless mistake

Algebra

Finding the center and radius of a circle

<u>Example problem</u>
Use completing the square to find the center and radius of a circle given by the polynomial equation:
$$x^2 + y^2 + 6x - 2y - 6 = 0$$

Rewrite the equation by grouping the x-terms and y-terms and moving the constant to the other side of the equation.
$$x^2 + y^2 + 6x - 2y - 6 = 0$$
$$(x^2 + 6x) + (y^2 - 2y) = 6$$
Prepare to complete the square by adding spaces in each set of parentheses and on the other side of the equation.
$$(x^2 + 6x + \_) + (y^2 - 2y + \_) = 6 + \_ + \_$$
For the x group: $\left(\frac{6}{2}\right)^2 = 3^2 = 9$ For the y group: $\left(\frac{2}{2}\right)^2 = 1^2 = 1$ Determine what is added to each group by dividing the middle coefficient by 2 and then squaring the result.
$$(x^2 + 6x + 9) + (y^2 - 2y + 1) = 6 + 9 + 1$$
Factor the groups and simplify the right side of the equation.
$$(x + 3)^2 + (y - 1)^2 = 16$$
Factor the groups and simplify the right side of the equation.
$$(x + 3)^2 + (y - 1)^2 = 16.$$
Identify h, k, and r.
$$x - h = x + 3 \rightarrow h = -3$$
$$y - k = y - 1 \rightarrow k = 1$$
$$r^2 = 16 \rightarrow r = 4$$
The center of the circle is (-3, 1), and the radius is 4.

Equation of a parabola

<u>Example problems</u>
Problem 1: Identify the equation of a parabola given a focus and directrix.
focus: (2,5) and directrix: $y = 1$

A parabola is the set of points equidistant from a point called the focus and line called the directrix, which does not pass through the focus. A parabola curves around the focus and away from the directrix but intersects neither. The vertex (h, k) of the parabola lies on the parabola's line of symmetry, which passes through the focus and is perpendicular to the directrix. Identify the orientation of the parabola. Since the directrix is a horizontal line represented by the equation $y = 1$, the parabola is oriented vertically and can therefore be represented by the equation $4p(y - k) = (x - h)^2$, where (h, k) is the vertex of the parabola and $(h, k + p)$ is the focus of the parabola. The vertex is halfway between the focus and the directrix, so find the mean of the y-values in the focus and directrix to find the vertex:

$\left(2, \frac{5+1}{2}\right) \rightarrow (2,3) = (h,k)$. The y-value of the focus, 5, is represented by $k + p$; $k = 3$, so $3 + p = 5 \rightarrow p = 2$. Substitute h, k, and p into the equation of a parabola: $4p(y - k) = (x - h)^2 \rightarrow 8(y - 3) = (x - 2)^2$.

Problem 2: Given a focus and directrix, identify the equation of a parabola.
focus: $(6, -2)$ and directrix: $x = 0$

A parabola is the set of points equidistant from a point called the focus and line called the directrix, which does not pass through the focus. A parabola curves around the focus and away from the directrix but intersects neither. The vertex (h, k) of the parabola lies on the parabola's line of symmetry, which passes through the focus and is perpendicular to the directrix. Identify the orientation of the parabola. Since the directrix is a vertical line represented by the equation $x = 0$, the parabola is oriented horizontally and can therefore be represented by the equation $4p(x - h) = (y - k)^2$, where (h, k) is the vertex of the parabola and $(h + p, k)$ is the focus of the parabola. The vertex is halfway between the focus and the directrix, so find the mean of the x-values in the focus and directrix to find the vertex: $\left(\frac{6+0}{2}, -2\right) \rightarrow$ $(3, -2)$. Compare the x-values in the vertex and the focus to find p: $p = 6 - 3 = 3$. Substitute h, k, and p into the equation of a parabola: $4p(x - h) = (y - k)^2 \rightarrow 12(x - 3) = (y + 2)^2$.

Equation of an ellipse

<u>Example problems</u>
Problem 1: Identify the equation of an ellipse with foci at $(5,3)$ and $(11,3)$ and a focal constant of 10.

An ellipse is the set of points around two foci such that the sum of the distances from any point on the ellipse to each focus is the focal constant. The center of the ellipse is equidistant from the foci and lies on the major axis. The orientation of the ellipse is also along the major axis. The ends of the major axis are called vertices. The ends of the minor axis are called co-vertices. Identify the orientation of the ellipse. The y-values are the same in both foci, so the major axis of the ellipse is at $y = 3$. Therefore, the ellipse is oriented horizontally. The equation for an ellipse with a horizontal major axis is $\frac{(x-h)^2}{a^2} + \frac{(y-k)^2}{b^2} = 1$, where (h, k) is the he center of the ellipse, a is half the focal constant, and a and b are related by the equation $a^2 - b^2 = c^2$, where c is the horizontal distance between the focus and the center. The center is the point along the major axis between the two foci: $\left(\frac{11+5}{2}, 3\right) \rightarrow$ $(8,3)$. Find the horizontal distance c between the focus and the center: $c = 11 - 8 = 3$. Divide the focal constant by 2 to find a: $a = \frac{10}{2} = 5$. Find b by using a, c, and the formula $a^2 - b^2 = c^2$: $5^2 - b^2 = 3^2 \rightarrow 25 - b^2 = 9 \rightarrow$ $b^2 = 25 - 9 = 16 \rightarrow b = 4$. Substitute a, b, h, and k into the equation of an ellipse: $\frac{(x-h)^2}{a^2} + \frac{(y-k)^2}{b^2} = 1 \rightarrow \frac{(x-8)^2}{5^2} + \frac{(y-3)^2}{4^2} = 1 \rightarrow \frac{(x-8)^2}{25} + \frac{(y-3)^2}{16} = 1$.

Problem 2: Identify the equation of an ellipse with foci at $(2,1)$ and $(2,5)$ and a focal constant of 5.

An ellipse is the set of points around two foci such that the sum of the distances from any point on the ellipse to each focus is the focal constant. The center of the ellipse is equidistant from the foci and lies on the major axis. The orientation of the ellipse is also along the major axis. The ends of the major axis are called vertices. The ends of the minor axis are called co-vertices. Identify the orientation of the ellipse. The x-values are the same in both foci, so the major axis of the ellipse is at $x = 2$. Therefore, the ellipse is oriented vertically. The equation for an ellipse with a horizontal major axis is $\frac{(x-h)^2}{b^2} + \frac{(y-k)^2}{a^2} = 1$, where (h, k) is the he center of the ellipse, a is half the focal constant, and a and b are related by the equation $a^2 - b^2 = c^2$, where c is the vertical distance between the focus and the center. The center is the point along the major axis between the two foci:: $\left(2, \frac{1+5}{2}\right) \rightarrow (2,3)$. Find the vertical distance c between the focus and the center: $c = 5 - 3 = 2$. Divide the focal constant by 2 to find a: $a = \frac{5}{2} = 2.5$. Find b by using a, c, and the formula $a^2 - b^2 = c^2$: $(2.5)^2 - b^2 = 2^2 \rightarrow 6.25 - b^2 = 4 \rightarrow b^2 = 6.25 - 4 = 2.25 \rightarrow b = 1.5$. Substitute a, b, h, and k into the equation of an ellipse: $\frac{(x-h)^2}{b^2} + \frac{(y-k)^2}{a^2} = 1 \rightarrow \frac{(x-2)^2}{1.5^2} + \frac{(y-3)^2}{2.5^2} = 1 \rightarrow \frac{(x-2)^2}{2.25} + \frac{(y-3)^2}{6.25} = 1 \rightarrow \frac{(x-2)^2}{\frac{9}{4}} + \frac{(y-3)^2}{\frac{25}{4}} = 1 \rightarrow \frac{4(x-2)^2}{9} + \frac{4(y-3)^2}{25} = 1$.

Equation of a hyperbola

<u>Example problems</u>
Problem 1: Identify the equation of a hyperbola given the foci $(-4,5)$ and $(6,5)$ and focal constant 8.

A hyperbola is the set of points whose distances from the foci are different by a constant (the focal constant). The foci are two points, one in each section of the hyperbola. The center, (h, k), is a point between the two sections of the hyperbola and is equidistant from the foci and along the major axis.
To find the equation of the hyperbola, first identify the orientation of the hyperbola. The foci lie along the line $y = 5$, so the hyperbola is orientated horizontally. The center is the point equidistant from the foci: $\left(\frac{-4+6}{2}, 5\right) \rightarrow$ $(1,5)$. Compare the x-values of the center and one focus to find c: $c = 1 - (-4) = 5$. Divide the focal constant by 2 to find a: $a = \frac{8}{2} = 4$. Find b by using a, c, and the formula $a^2 + b^2 = c^2$: $4^2 + b^2 = 5^2 \rightarrow 16 + b^2 = 25 \rightarrow b^2 = 25 - 16 = 9 \rightarrow b = 3$. Substitute a, b, h, and k into the equation of a horizontally oriented hyperbola: $\frac{(x-h)^2}{a^2} - \frac{(y-k)^2}{b^2} = 1 \rightarrow \frac{(x-1)^2}{4^2} - \frac{(y-5)^2}{3^2} = 1 \rightarrow \frac{(x-1)^2}{16} - \frac{(y-5)^2}{9} = 1$.

Problem 2: Identify the equation of a hyperbola with foci at $(-2, -4)$ and $(-2, 22)$ and a focal constant of 10.

A hyperbola is the set of points whose distances from the foci are different by a constant (the focal constant). The foci are two points, one in each section of the hyperbola. The center, (h, k), is a point between the two sections of the hyperbola and is equidistant from the foci and along the major axis.

To find the equation of the hyperbola, first identify the orientation of the hyperbola. The foci lie along the line $x = -2$, so the hyperbola is orientated vertically. The center is the point equidistant from the foci: $\left(-2, \frac{-4+22}{2}\right) \rightarrow$ $(-2, 9)$. Compare the y-values of the center and one focus to find c: $c = 22 - 9 = 13$. Divide the focal constant by 2 to find a: $a = \frac{10}{2} = 5$. Find b by using a, c, and the formula $a^2 + b^2 = c^2$: $5^2 + b^2 = 13^2 \rightarrow 25 + b^2 = 169 \rightarrow b^2 = 169 - 25 = 144 \rightarrow b = 12$. Substitute a, b, h, and k into the equation of a vertically oriented hyperbola: $\frac{(y-k)^2}{a^2} - \frac{(x-h)^2}{b^2} = 1 \rightarrow \frac{(y-9)^2}{5^2} - \frac{(x+2)^2}{12^2} = 1 \rightarrow \frac{(y-9)^2}{25} - \frac{(x+2)^2}{144} = 1$.

Equation of a circle

Example problems

Problem 1: Derive the equation of a circle with a given center and radius using the Pythagorean Theorem.

Given is a circle with center (h, k) and radius r. Point (x, y) is on the circle. Use the Pythagorean Theorem to determine a relationship between the distance r and the points (h, k) and (x, y). In the right triangle, the length of the horizontal leg is $(x - h)$ and the length of the vertical leg is $(y - k)$. The Pythagorean Theorem states that the square of the hypotenuse is equal to the sum of the squares of the legs, or $(x - h)^2 + (y - k)^2 = r^2$. This equation defines the circle with center (h, k), radius r, and point (x, y) on the circle.

Problem 2: Find the equation of a circle with center $(-2, 8)$ and radius $r = 6$ using the Pythagorean Theorem.

Given a circle with center $(-2, 8)$ and radius $r = 6$. Point (x, y) is on the circle.
Use the Pythagorean Theorem to determine a relationship between the distance $r = 6$ and the points $(-2, 8)$ and (x, y). In the right triangle, the length of the horizontal leg is $(x + 2)$ and the length of the vertical leg is $(y - 8)$. The Pythagorean Theorem states that the square of the hypotenuse is equal to the sum of the squares of the legs, or $(x - h)^2 + (y - k)^2 = r^2 \rightarrow (x + 2)^2 + (y - 8)^2 = 6^2 \rightarrow (x + 2)^2 + (y - 8)^2 = 36$.

Determining whether a quadrilateral is a rectangle

Example problems

Problem 1: Determine whether or not the quadrilateral defined by $A(5,4)$, $B(-4,3)$, $C(-4,1)$, and $D(5,1)$ is a rectangle.

A rectangle has two pairs of congruent opposite sides and four right angles. To find the lengths of the sides, use the distance formula,

$$d = \sqrt{(x_1 - x_2)^2 + (y_1 - y_2)^2}.$$

AB	BC
$\sqrt{[5 - (-4)]^2 + (4 - 3)^2}$	$\sqrt{[-4 - (-4)]^2 + (3 - 1)^2}$
$\sqrt{(9)^2 + (1)^2}$	$\sqrt{(0)^2 + (2)^2}$
$\sqrt{81 + 1}$	$\sqrt{0 + 4}$
$\sqrt{82}$	$\sqrt{4} = 2$
CD	DA
$\sqrt{(-4 - 5)^2 + (1 - 1)^2}$	$\sqrt{(5 - 5)^2 + (1 - 4)^2}$
$\sqrt{(-9)^2 + (0)^2}$	$\sqrt{(0)^2 + (-3)^2}$
$\sqrt{81 + 0}$	$\sqrt{0 + 9}$
$\sqrt{81} = 9$	$\sqrt{9} = 3$

Since AB ≠ CD and BC ≠ DA, Quadrilateral ABCD is not a rectangle, and no further testing is required.

Problem 2: Determine whether or not the quadrilateral defined by $A(8, -1)$, $B(-2, -1)$, $C(-2,6)$, and $D(8,6)$ is a rectangle.

A rectangle has 2 pairs of congruent opposite sides and 4 right angles. To find the lengths of the sides, use the distance formula,

$$d = \sqrt{(x_1 - x_2)^2 + (y_1 - y_2)^2}.$$

AB	BC
$\sqrt{[8 - (-2)]^2 + [-1 - (-1)]^2}$	$\sqrt{[-2 - (-2)]^2 + (-1 - 6)^2}$
$\sqrt{(10)^2 + (0)^2}$ or $\sqrt{100 + 0}$	$\sqrt{(0)^2 + (-7)^2}$ o $\sqrt{0 + 49}$
$\sqrt{100} = 10$	$\sqrt{49} = 7$
CD	DA
$\sqrt{(-2 - 8)^2 + (6 - 6)^2}$	$\sqrt{(8 - 8)^2 + [6 - (-1)]^2}$
$\sqrt{(-10)^2 + (0)^2}$ or	$\sqrt{(0)^2 + (7)^2}$ or $\sqrt{0 + 49}$
$\sqrt{100 + 0}$	$\sqrt{49} = 7$
$\sqrt{100} = 10$	

Since AB = CD & BC = DA, Test to see if quadrilateral ABCD is a rectangle. To find if the angles are right angles, find the slopes of the four sides. Perpendicular sides will have opposite, inverse slopes.

$\underline{AB}$ $m = \dfrac{(-1)-(-1)}{(-2)-8} = \dfrac{0}{-10} = 0$			$\underline{BC}$ $m = \dfrac{6-(-1)}{(-2)-(-2)} = \dfrac{7}{0} = undef$		
$\underline{CD}$ $m = \dfrac{6-6}{8-(-2)} = \dfrac{0}{10} = 0$			$\underline{DA}$ $m = \dfrac{(-1)-6}{(-2)-(-2)} = \dfrac{-7}{0} = undef$		

Although $\overline{BC}$ and $\overline{DA}$ have undefined slopes, they are perpendicular to $\overline{AB}$ and $\overline{CD}$ because lines with undefined slopes are perpendicular to lines with slopes of 0.

Point on a circle

Example problems
Problem 1: Determine whether or not the point $(3, 3\sqrt{3})$ lies on the circle which is centered at the origin and which contains the point $(0,6)$.

A circle consists of all points in a plane that are a given distance from the center. One way to determine whether a point lies on a particular circle is to find the distance between the center of the circle and the point, and compare it to the radius of the circle. If they are the same, then the point lies on the circle.
Begin by finding the radius of the circle:
$$r = \sqrt{(6-0)^2 + (0-0)^2} = \sqrt{36} = 6$$
If the point $(3, 3\sqrt{3})$ is also 6 units from the circle's center, then it lies on the circle.
$$d = \sqrt{(3-0)^2 + \left(3\sqrt{3}-0\right)^2} = \sqrt{9+27} = \sqrt{36} = 6$$
Therefore, point $(3, 3\sqrt{3})$ lies on the given circle.

Problem 2: Determine whether or not the point $(1,2)$ lies on the circle which is centered at the origin and which contains the point $(\sqrt{2}, \sqrt{2})$.

A circle consists of all points in a plane that are a given distance from the center. One way to determine whether a point lies on a particular circle is to find the distance between the center of the circle and the point, and compare it to the radius of the circle. If they are the same, then the point lies on the circle.
Begin by finding the radius of the circle:
$$r = \sqrt{\left(\sqrt{2}-0\right)^2 + \left(\sqrt{2}-0\right)^2} = \sqrt{2+2} = \sqrt{4} = 2$$
If the point $(1,2)$ is also 2 units from the circle's center, then it lies on the circle.
$$d = \sqrt{(1-0)^2 + (2-0)^2} = \sqrt{1+4} = \sqrt{5} \neq 2$$
Therefore, point $(1,2)$ does not lie on the given circle.

Using slope-intercept form

Example problems
Problem 1: Show that the lines given by equations $5y + 2x = 7$ and $10y + 4x = 28$ are parallel.

- 8 -

Parallel lines are two lines which have the same slope and do not intersect. To determine whether $5y + 2x = 7$ and $10y + 4x = 28$ are parallel, first find the slope of each line by rewriting in slope-intercept form: $5y = -2x + 7 \rightarrow y = \frac{-2}{5}x + \frac{7}{5}$; $10y = -4x + 28 \rightarrow y = \frac{-4}{10}x + \frac{28}{10} \rightarrow y = \frac{-2}{5}x + \frac{14}{5}$. The two lines have same slope. To show the lines do not intersect, show that there is no solution to the system formed by the given equations. $\frac{-2}{5}x + \frac{7}{5} = \frac{-2}{5}x + \frac{14}{5} \rightarrow \frac{7}{5} = \frac{14}{5}$. When the solution of a system of equations results in a false statement, the solution is the empty set; there is no point contained by both lines, so the lines do not intersect.

Problem 2: Show that the lines given by equations $y - 3x = 5$ and $3y + x = -6$ are perpendicular.

When two lines have slopes which are negative reciprocals of each other. $(m_1 \cdot m_2 = -1)$, they are perpendicular, which means they meet at right angles.

Find the slope of the given two lines, $y - 3x = 5$ and $3y + x = -6$, by rewriting in slope-intercept form: $y = 3x + 5$; $3y = -x - 6 \rightarrow y = \frac{-1}{3}x - \frac{6}{3} \rightarrow y = \frac{-1}{3}x - 2$. The two lines have slopes $m_1 = 3$ and $m_2 = \frac{-1}{3}$, which are negative reciprocals. Therefore, the lines are perpendicular.

Problem 3: Find the equation of the line passing through $(-2,6)$ and parallel to $5y - 15x = -25$.

Parallel lines have the same slopes.

Given equation: $5y - 15x = -25$ $\quad 5y = 15x - 25$ $\quad\quad y = 3x - 5$ Slope: $m_1 = 3 = m_2$	Solution equation: $y = m \cdot x + b$ $(y = 6, m_2 = 3, x = -2)$ $6 = 3 \cdot (-2) + b$ $6 = -6 + b$ $12 = b$ ----------------------------------- $y = 3x + 12$ $y - 3x = 12$

The line passing through $(-2,6)$ and parallel to $5y - 15x = -25$ is $y - 3x = 12$.

Problem 4: Find the equation of the line passing through $(9, -1)$ and perpendicular to $-2y + 3x = 5$.

Perpendicular lines have opposite, inverse slopes.

Given equation:	Solution equation:
$-2y + 3x = 5$	$y = m \cdot x + b$
$\quad -2y = -3x + 5$	$(y = -1, m_2 = \frac{-2}{3}, x = 9)$
$\quad y = \dfrac{-3}{-2}x + 5$	$-1 = \dfrac{-2}{3} \cdot 9 + b$
$\quad y = \dfrac{3}{2}x + 5$	$-1 = -6 + b$
Slope: $m_1 = \dfrac{3}{2}$	$5 = b$
$\quad m_1 \cdot m_2 = -1$	- -
$\quad \dfrac{3}{2} \cdot m_2 = -1$	$y = \dfrac{-2}{3} \cdot x + 5$
$\quad m_2 = \dfrac{-2}{3}$	$3y = -2x + 15$
	$3y + 2x = 15$

The line passing through $(9, -1)$ and perpendicular to $-2y + 3x = 5$ is $3y + 2x = 15$.

Point that partitions a line segment

<u>Example problems</u>
Problem 1: Describe how to find the point that partitions a given line segment into two segments with a given length ratio.

Given two points, (x_1, y_1) and (x_2, y_2) and the ratio $a: b$.

steps:	x-values:	y-values:
1. find the difference between the values	$d_x = x_2 - x_1$	$d_y = y_2 - y_1$
2. find the fraction that represents the ratio	$a: b \rightarrow \dfrac{a}{a+b}$ this is the fraction of difference between x_1 and x_3	$a: b \rightarrow \dfrac{a}{a+b}$ this is also the fraction of difference between y_1 and y_3
3. find the difference between the first point and the partition point, multiply the fraction and the differences between x_1 and x_2 and y_1 and y_2	$m = \dfrac{a}{a+b} \cdot d_x$	$n = \dfrac{a}{a+b} \cdot d_y$
4. find the partition point by adding the differences to the first point	$x_3 = x_1 + m$	$y_3 = y_1 + n$

Problem 2: Describe and execute the steps to find the point that partitions the line segment between $(3,4)$ and $(7,12)$ into two segments with a length ratio of $1:3$.

Given two points, $(3,4)$ and $(7,12)$ and ratio $1:3$.

steps:	x-values:	y-values:
1. find the difference between the values	$d_x = 7 - 3$ $= 4$	$d_y = 12 - 4$ $= 8$
2. find the fraction that represents the ratio	$1:3 \rightarrow$ $\frac{1}{1+3} = \frac{1}{4}$ this is the fraction of difference between x_1 and x_3	$1:3 \rightarrow \frac{1}{1+3} = \frac{1}{4}$ this is also the fraction of difference between y_1 and y_3
3. find the difference between the first point and the partition point, multiply the fraction and the differences between x_1 and x_2 and y_1 and y_2	$m = \frac{1}{4} \cdot$ $4 = 1$	$n = \frac{1}{4} \cdot 8 = 2$
4. find the partition point by adding the differences to the first point	$x_3 = 3 + 1$ $= 4$	$y_3 = 4 + 2 = 6$

The partition point is $(4,6)$.

Problem 3: Describe and execute the steps to find the point that partitions the line segment between $(-3,5)$ and $(3,-7)$ into two segments with a length ratio of $5:1$.

Given two points, $(-3,5)$ and $(3,-7)$ and ratio $5:1$.

steps:	x-values:	y-values:
1. Find the difference between the values	d_x $= 3 - (-3)$ $= 6$	$d_y = (-7) - 5$ $= -12$
2. Find the fraction that represents the ratio	$5:1 \rightarrow \frac{5}{5+1} =$ $\frac{5}{6}$ this is the fraction of difference between x_1 & x_3	$5:1 \rightarrow \frac{5}{5+1} = \frac{5}{6}$ this is also the fraction of difference between y_1 and y_3

3. find the difference between the first point & the partition point, multiply the fraction & the differences between x_1 & x_2 & y_1 & y_2	$m = \frac{5}{6} \cdot 6 = 5$	$n = \frac{5}{6} \cdot (-12) = -10$
4. find the partition point by adding the differences to the first point	$x_3 = -3 + 5$ $= 2$	$y_3 = 5 + (-10)$ $= -5$

The partition point is $(2, -5)$.

Using coordinates to find perimeter and area

To use coordinates to find the perimeter of a figure, find the distance between all vertices. Add all the distances together.

$$d_{AB} = \sqrt{(x_B - x_A)^2 + (y_B - y_A)^2}$$

To use coordinates to find the area of a figure, find the critical distances. Use the appropriate formula.

for TRIANGLES: find the *BASE* and the *HEIGHT* **the height may not be along the side of the triangle** use the formula: $AREA = \frac{1}{2} \cdot BASE \cdot HEIGHT$	for RECTANGLES: find the *LENGTH* and the *WIDTH* use the formula: $AREA = LENGTH \cdot WIDTH$

<u>Example problems</u>
Problem 1: Find the perimeter of the figure given by the points $A(5,4)$, $B(3,-1)$, and $C(7,-1)$.

$$d_{AB} = \sqrt{(3-5)^2 + (-1-4)^2} = \sqrt{(-2)^2 + (-5)^2} = \sqrt{4 + 25} = \sqrt{29}$$
$$d_{BC} = \sqrt{(7-3)^2 + [-1-(-1)]^2} = \sqrt{(4)^2 + (0)^2} = \sqrt{16 + 0} = \sqrt{16} = 4$$
$$d_{CA} = \sqrt{(5-7)^2 + [4-(-1)]^2} = \sqrt{(-2)^2 + (5)^2} = \sqrt{4 + 25} = \sqrt{29}$$
Perimeter: $d_{AB} + d_{BC} + d_{CA} = \sqrt{29} + 4 + \sqrt{29} = 4 + 2\sqrt{29}$.

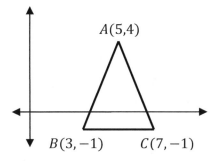

$A(5,4)$

$B(3,-1)$ $C(7,-1)$

Problem 2: Find the perimeter of the figure given by the points $A(7,11)$, $B(3,3)$, $C(9,0)$ and $D(13,8)$.

$$d_{AB} = \sqrt{(3-7)^2 + (3-11)^2} = \sqrt{(-4)^2 + (-8)^2} = \sqrt{16 + 64} = \sqrt{80} = 4\sqrt{5}$$
$$d_{BC} = \sqrt{(9-3)^2 + (0-3)^2} = \sqrt{(6)^2 + (-3)^2} = \sqrt{36 + 9} = \sqrt{45} = 3\sqrt{5}$$
$$d_{CD} = \sqrt{(13-9)^2 + (8-0)^2} = \sqrt{(4)^2 + (8)^2} = \sqrt{16 + 64} = \sqrt{80} = 4\sqrt{5}$$
$$d_{DA} = \sqrt{(7-13)^2 + (11-8)^2} = \sqrt{(-6)^2 + (3)^2} = \sqrt{36 + 9} = \sqrt{45} = 3\sqrt{5}$$

Perimeter: $d_{AB} + d_{BC} + d_{CD} + d_{DA} = 4\sqrt{5} + 3\sqrt{5} + 4\sqrt{5} + 3\sqrt{5} = 2(4\sqrt{5}) + 2(3\sqrt{5}) = 8\sqrt{5} + 6\sqrt{5} = 14\sqrt{5}$.

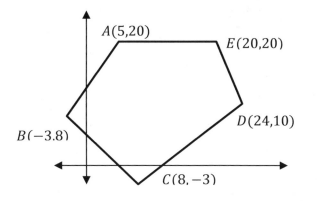

$A(5,20)$ $E(20,20)$

$B(-3.8)$

$D(24,10)$

$C(8,-3)$

Problem 3: Find the area of the figure given by the points $A(5,4)$, $B(3,-1)$, and $C(7,-1)$.

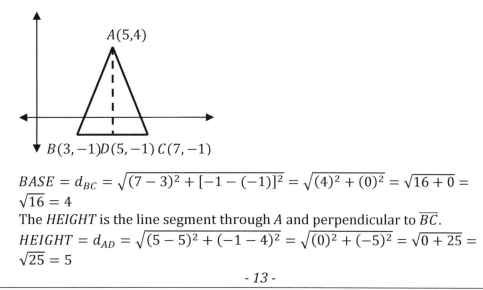

$A(5,4)$

$B(3,-1)$ $D(5,-1)$ $C(7,-1)$

$BASE = d_{BC} = \sqrt{(7-3)^2 + [-1-(-1)]^2} = \sqrt{(4)^2 + (0)^2} = \sqrt{16+0} = \sqrt{16} = 4$

The *HEIGHT* is the line segment through A and perpendicular to $\overline{BC}$.

$HEIGHT = d_{AD} = \sqrt{(5-5)^2 + (-1-4)^2} = \sqrt{(0)^2 + (-5)^2} = \sqrt{0+25} = \sqrt{25} = 5$

- 13 -

$$AREA = \frac{1}{2} \cdot BASE \cdot HEIGHT = \frac{1}{2} \cdot 4 \cdot 5 = \frac{1}{2} \cdot 20 = 10$$
The area of the triangle is 10 square units.

Problem 4: Find the area of the figure given by the points $A(7,11)$, $B(3,3)$, and $C(13,8)$.

$$BASE = d_{AC} = \sqrt{(13-7)^2 + (8-11)^2} = \sqrt{(6)^2 + (-3)^2} = \sqrt{36+9} =$$
$$\sqrt{45} = 3\sqrt{5}$$
$\overline{AC} \perp \overline{AB}$ because $m_{AB} \cdot m_{AC} = \frac{11-8}{7-13} \cdot \frac{11-3}{7-3} = \frac{3}{-6} \cdot \frac{8}{4} = \frac{24}{-24} = -1.$
$$HEIGHT = d_{AB} = \sqrt{(3-7)^2 + (3-11)^2} = \sqrt{(-4)^2 + (-8)^2} = \sqrt{16+64} =$$
$$\sqrt{80} = 4\sqrt{5}$$
$$AREA = \frac{1}{2} \cdot BASE \cdot HEIGHT = \frac{1}{2} \cdot 3\sqrt{5} \cdot 4\sqrt{5} = \frac{1}{2} \cdot 12 \cdot 5 =$$
$\frac{1}{2} \cdot 60 = 30$ The area of the triangle is 30 square units.

Problem 5: Find the area of the figure given by the points $A(7,11)$, $B(3,3)$, $C(9,0)$ and $D(13,8)$.

$$LENGTH = d_{AB} = \sqrt{(3-7)^2 + (3-11)^2} = \sqrt{(-4)^2 + (-8)^2} = \sqrt{16+64} =$$
$$\sqrt{80} = 4\sqrt{5}$$
$\overline{AB} \perp \overline{AD}$ because $m_{AB} \cdot m_{AD} = \frac{11-3}{7-3} \cdot \frac{11-8}{7-13} = \frac{8}{4} \cdot \frac{3}{-6} = \frac{24}{-24} = -1.$
$$WIDTH = d_{AD} = \sqrt{(13-7)^2 + (8-11)^2} = \sqrt{(6)^2 + (-3)^2} =$$
$$\sqrt{36+9} = \sqrt{45} = 3\sqrt{5}$$
$$AREA = LENGTH \cdot WIDTH = 4\sqrt{5} \cdot 3\sqrt{5} = 12 \cdot 5 = 60$$
The area of the rectangle is 60 square units.

Data Analysis and Probability

Dot plot, histogram, and box plot

Dot plots, histograms, and box plots are three different methods of representing data sets in graphical form. While they all have similar purposes, some are more suitable for some data sets than others. Dot plots represent each data point as a separate dot, and are most useful for relatively small data sets with a small number of possible values. When the data set contains more than a few dozen points, dot plots may become unwieldy. For larger data sets, where the data distribution is continuous rather than discrete, histograms may be more practical. Histograms are especially useful to estimate the *density* of the data, and to estimate probability density functions. Box plots may be used to summarize the shape of a larger number of univariate data values; they are most useful for comparing separate groups of data, such as the results of several different experiments, or the statistics of several discrete populations.

Dot plot
A dot plot is a representation of a data set in which each data point is represented by a dot or similar marking, with matching data points grouped in columns. For instance, the data set {2, 1, 3, 1, 1, 5, 4, 4, 3, 3, 3, 4, 1, 5} can be represented as a dot plot as follows:

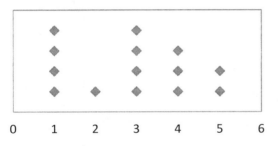

For large data sets, it is possible for each dot in a dot plot to represent more than one data point. However, for such data sets other representations may be more suitable.

Histogram
A histogram is a representation of a data set in which the data are represented by bars corresponding to discrete intervals, with the height of each bar representative of the number of data points falling in the corresponding interval. For example, the data set {101, 141, 105, 159, 122, 107, 145, 153, 183, 172, 164, 162, 144, 132, 138, 116, 155, 147, 141, 129, 168, 145, 152} can be represented by a histogram as follows:

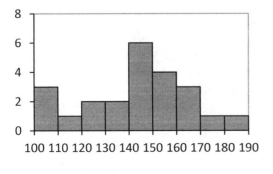

Histograms are useful for large data sets with values that may range continuously over intervals rather than being confined to discrete possibilities.

Box plot

A *box plot*, or box-and-whisker plot, is a representation of one or more data sets in which each data set is represented by a box with a bar in the middle and a "whisker" on each side. The bar represents the *median* of the data, and the edges of the box represent the first and third quartiles. The ends of the whiskers may represent the maximum and minimum data values, although often outliers are excluded and are represented instead as discrete points.

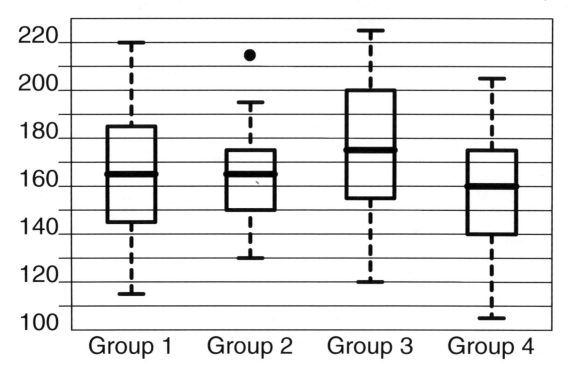

For example, given the data, 5, 5, 6, 9, 12, 14, 15, 17, 17, 21, 24, 26, 29, 31, 36, 38, 39, 46, 47, 49, the following summary statistics may be recorded: Median = 22.5, Q1 = 13, Q3 = 37, minimum = 5, and maximum = 49. Thus, a box plot of this data will show a box, with a middle bar at the value, 22.5, edges of the box at the values, 13 and 37, and whiskers at the values, 5 and 49. Box plots are useful when it is desired to compare the statistics of multiple related data sets, such as several different groups of experimental subjects.

Mean

The mean is the average of the data points; that is, it is the sum of the data points divided by the number of data points. Mathematically, the mean of a set of data points $\{x_1, x_2, x_3, \ldots x_n\}$ can be written as $\bar{X} = \sum \frac{X}{N}$. For instance, for the data set (1, 3, 6, 8, 100, 800), the mean is $\frac{1+3+6+8+100+800}{6} = 153$.

The mean is most useful, when data is approximately normal and does not include extreme outliers. In the above example, the data shows much variation. Thus, the mean is not the best measure of central tendency to use, when interpreting the data. With this data set, the median will give a more complete picture of the distribution.

Median

The median is the value in the middle of the data set, in the sense that 50% of the data points lie above the median and 50% of the data points lie below. The median can be determined by simply putting the data points in order, and selecting the data point in the middle. If there is an even number of data points, then the median is the average of the middle two data points. For instance, for the data set {1, 3, 6, 8, 100, 800}, the median is $\frac{6+8}{2} = 7$.

For distributions with widely varying data points, especially those with large outliers, the median is a more appropriate measure of central tendency, and thus gives a better idea of a "typical" data point. Notice in the data set above, the mean is 153, while the median is 7.

Mode

The mode is the value that appears most often in the data set. For instance, for the data set {2, 6, 4, 9, 4, 5, 7, 6, 4, 1, 5, 6, 7, 5, 6}, the mode is 6: the number 6 appears four times in the data set, while the next most frequent values, 4 and 5, appear only three times each. It is possible for a data set to have more than one mode: in the data set {11, 14, 17, 16, 11, 17, 12, 14, 17, 14, 13}, 14 and 17 are both modes, appearing three times each. In the extreme case of a uniform distribution—a distribution in which all values appear with equal probability—*all* values in the data set are modes.

The mode is useful to get a general sense of the shape of the distribution; it shows where the peaks of the distribution are. More information is necessary to get a more detailed description of the full shape.

First quartile

The first quartile of a data set is a value greater than or equal to one quarter of the data points (and less than the other three quarters). Various methods exist for defining the first quartile precisely; one of the simplest is to define the first quartile as the median of the first half of the ordered data (excluding the median if there are an odd number of data points). Applying this method, for example, to the data set {3, 1, 12, 7, 17, 4, 10, 8, 9, 20, 4}, we proceed as follows: Putting the data in order, we get {1, 3, 4, 4, 7, 8, 9, 10, 12, 17, 20}. The first half (excluding the median) is {1, 3, 4, 4, 7}, which has a median of 4. Therefore the first quartile of this data set is 4.

Third quartile

The third quartile of a data set is a value greater than or equal to three quarters of the data points (and less than the remaining quarter). Various methods exist for defining the third quartiles precisely; one of the simplest is to define the third quartile as the median of the second half of the ordered data (excluding the median if there are an odd number of data points).

Applying this method, for example, to the data set {3, 1, 12, 7, 17, 4, 10, 8, 9, 20, 4}, we proceed as follows: Putting the data in order, we get {1, 3, 4, 4, 7, 8, 9, 10, 12, 17, 20}. The second half (excluding the median) is {9, 10, 12, 17, 20}, which has a median of 12. Therefore the third quartile of this data set is 12.

Interquartile range

The interquartile range of a data set is the difference between the third and first quartiles. That is, one quarter of the data fall below the interquartile range and one quarter of the data above it. Exactly half of the data points fall within the interquartile range, half of those above the median and half below. (This is, of course, why the quartile points are called "quartiles", because they divide the data into quarters: one quarter of the data points are below the first quartile, one quarter between the first and second quartile (the median), and so on.)

The interquartile range is useful to get a rough idea of the spread of the data. The median by itself shows where the data are centered (or rather, shows one measure of central tendency); the interquartile range gives a better idea of how much the data points vary from this center.

Standard deviation

The standard deviation of a data set is a measurement of how much the data points vary from the mean. More precisely, it is equal to the square root of the average of the squares of the differences between each point and the mean: $s_x = \sqrt{\frac{\Sigma(X-\bar{X})^2}{N-1}}$.

The standard deviation is useful for determining the spread, or dispersion, of the data, or how far they vary from the mean. The smaller the standard deviation, the closer the values tend to be to the mean; the larger the standard deviation, the more they tend to be scattered far from the mean.

Outlier

An outlier is an extremely high or extremely low value in the data set. It may be the result of measurement error, in which case, the outlier is not a valid member of the data set. However, it may also be a valid member of the distribution. Unless a measurement error is identified, the experimenter cannot know for certain if an outlier is or is not a member of the distribution. There are arbitrary methods that can be employed to designate an extreme value as an outlier. One method designates an outlier (or possible outlier) to be any value less than $Q_1 - 1.5(IQR)$ or any value greater than $Q_3 + 1.5(IQR)$, where Q_1 and Q_3 are the first and third quartiles and IQR is the interquartile range. For instance, in the data set {42, 71, 22, 500, 33, 38, 62, 44, 58, 37, 61, 25}, the point 500 may be considered an outlier, since 500 is greater than 101.25 (61.5 + 1.5(26.5) = 101.25).

Regarding measurements of the center, outliers tend to have little or no effect on the mode, and in general little effect on the median, though their effects may be magnified for very small distributions. Means, however, are very sensitive to outliers; a single data point that lies far outside the range of the others may leave the mode and median almost unchanged while drastically altering the mean. For instance, the data set {2, 2, 5, 5, 5, 8, 11} has a mode and median of 5 and a mean of approximately 5.4; adding the outlying value 650 to the data set leaves the mode and median unchanged but increases the mean to 86. Like the median, the interquartile range is little affected by outliers, though, again, the effect may be greater for small data sets. The standard deviation, like the mean, is much more sensitive to outliers, and may be significantly increased by a single outlier that lies far from the spread of the rest of the points.

Shape of a measurement and its measures of central tendency

The measurement of central tendency with the most clearly visible relationship to the shape is the mode. The mode defines the peak of the distribution, and a distribution with multiple modes has multiple peaks. The relationship of the shape to the other measurements of central tendency is more subtle. For a symmetrical distribution with a single peak, the mode, median, and mean all coincide. For a distribution skewed to the left or right, however, this is not generally the case. One rule of thumb often given is that the median is displaced from the mode in the same direction as the skew of the graph, and the mean in the same direction farther still.

Two data sets with the same center but different spreads

It's certainly possible for two data sets to have the same center but different spreads; all that's necessary is for the points in one set to be clustered closer to the center than the other. Consider, for instance, two data sets that both have the normal distribution with the same mean but different standard deviations: all usual measurements of central tendency would match—the mean, mode, and median—but their spread, as measured by either interquartile range or by standard deviation, would differ. The following graph shows the distributions of two such data sets:

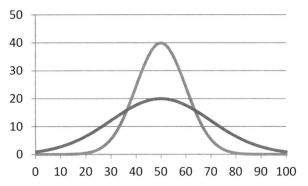

Two data sets with the same spread but different centers

It's certainly possible for two data sets to have the same spread but different centers; nothing prevents the data points of two sets from being equally near the center even if the center differs. Consider, for instance, two data sets that both have the normal distribution with the same standard deviation but different means: their spread, as measured by either interquartile range or by standard deviation, would match, but the measures of central tendency, mean, mode, and median—would differ between the data sets. The graph below shows the distributions of two such data sets:

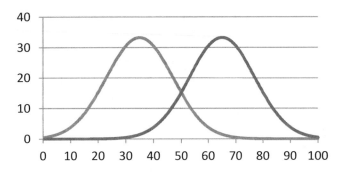

Two data distributions with the same spread and center but different shapes

It's certainly possible for two data distributions to have the same spread and center but different shapes. While the spread and the center are significant characteristics of a distribution, they are not sufficient to uniquely determine the distribution; two distributions may very well have the same spread and center but differ in the details. Consider, for instance, the data sets {5, 10, 15, 20, 25, 30, 35} and {7, 10, 11, 20, 29, 30, 33}: both these data sets have a mean and median of 20, an interquartile range of 20, and a standard deviation of approximately 10.8; yet clearly they are not identical, and have different shapes. For another example, consider an asymmetric distribution reflected about its mean; despite their different shapes, the distribution and its reflection have the same mean and necessarily the same spread.

Normal distribution

A normal distribution is a symmetrical, bell-shaped distribution that can be used to model real-world situations. In particular, the normal distribution is a good match for data that represents the sum or the mean of a large number of similar variables acting independently. If you roll a large number of dice, for instance, their mean will tend to follow close to a normal distribution.

The normal distribution has a number of useful properties. Perhaps the most notable is that the distribution of the sum or difference of two variables each of which follows the normal distributions is itself another normal distribution, with the mean equal to the sum or difference of the means of the distributions of the original variables, and the standard deviation equal to the square root of the sum of the squares of the standard deviations of the original distributions.

Fitting data to a normal distribution

The normal distribution is defined by the normal equation, $f(x) = \frac{1}{\sigma\sqrt{2\pi}} e^{-\frac{1}{2}\left(\frac{x-\mu}{\sigma}\right)^2}$, where μ is the mean and σ is the standard deviation. Generating a normal equation corresponding to a given mean and standard deviation, then, is as simple as putting the appropriate values for μ and σ into this equation. A standard deviation with a mean of 100 and a standard deviation of 10, for instance, would have a normal equation $f(x) = \frac{1}{10\sqrt{2\pi}} e^{-\frac{1}{2}\left(\frac{x-100}{10}\right)^2}$. The probability that the data lies within a certain range can be found by determining the area under the normal curve—the graph of the normal function—within the given range.

It's often simpler, however, to consider the *standard normal distribution*, with the equation $f(z) = \frac{1}{\sqrt{2\pi}} e^{-\frac{1}{2}z^2}$. This is simply a normal distribution with a mean of 0 and a standard deviation of 1. A standard z-distribution is represented by the formula, $z = \frac{X-\mu}{\sigma}$.

Many data sets that arise in real-world problems can be fit to or at least approximated by a normal distribution, and given the useful properties of this distribution it's often useful to do so. However, the normal distribution is not a good fit for all data sets. In general, if a data set seems to follow a symmetrical bell curve, it is likely (though not necessarily the case) that it can be usefully fit to a normal distribution. For a data sets that is clearly skewed and asymmetrical, however, such a fit is not suitable. Nor is it appropriate to try to fit to a normal distribution data sets that have no peaks, or multiple peaks (though it may be possible to fit such data to a *sum* of normal distributions).

Estimating population percentages in a normal distribution

The population percentages falling within certain ranges in a normal distribution can be estimated by finding the area under the normal curve. This can either be estimated by inspection or determined using a calculator. For certain values, however, the population percentages can be estimated more directly. About 68% of the data points in a normal distribution lie within one standard deviation of the mean, about 95% within two standard deviations, and about 99.9% within three. For a normal distribution with a mean of 100 and a standard deviation of 10, for instance, we would expect 68% of the data points to lie between 90 and 110 (100 ± 10), and 95% of the data points to lie between 80 and 120. Because of the normal distribution's symmetry, half of these would lie on each side of the mean, so, for instance, about 34% of the data points would lie between 90 and 100 and 34% between 100 and 110; about 2.5% of the data points (½(100% – 95%)) would exceed 120.

Estimating the area under a normal curve

Calculator
Most scientific calculators have statistical functions that allow the easy calculation of probabilities related to common probability distributions, including the normal distribution. The details depend on the particular model of calculator. In the TI-84, one of the most commonly used calculators today, the appropriate function can be accessed from the DISTR button (press "2nd", and then "VARS"). This will bring up a menu of distribution-related functions; select "normalcdf". The parameters of this function are, in order, the lower bound, the upper bound, the mean, and the standard deviation. For a normal distribution with a mean of 100 and a standard deviation of 10, for instance, to find the probability that a data point lies between 105 and 115 you would enter "normalcdf(105, 115, 100, 10)", yielding an answer of about 0.242, or 24.2%. If you desire to see the area visually, you can hit the right arrow from the DISTR menu to get to the DRAW menu, and choose "ShadeNorm". The parameters are the same as for the "normalcdf" function.

Spreadsheet
Most modern spreadsheet programs include functions that allow the user to find the area under a normal curve. In Microsoft Excel, the appropriate function is NORMDIST, which gives the total area of the graph to the left of a particular value. The first parameter of this function is the value in question, the second is the mean, and the third the standard

deviation. The fourth parameter should be simply set to TRUE. (If it's set to FALSE, Excel will return the value of the normal function at that point rather than the area under the curve.) For instance, for a normal distribution with a mean of 100 and a standard deviation of 10, to find the area under the curve to the left of 115, you would enter into the cell "=NORMDIST(115,100,10,TRUE)".

To find the area within a given interval, you can simply take the difference of two results. For instance, for the previous example, the area of the curve between 105 and 115 would be generated by "=NORMDIST(115,100,10,TRUE)-NORMDIST(105,100,10,TRUE)".

Table

Z-tables are available and give the total area under a normal curve to the left of a given value (or the larger portion). The area within an interval can be found by taking the difference between the areas for the right and left endpoints. A mean to z table is also available and may be used to find the area between the mean and a given value. This table may also be used, in order to find the area to the left (or right) or a value, by adding half the area under the normal curve (0.5), to the mean to z area represented by the given value. Z-tables represent standardized values. The raw values are not represented by the table. Instead, the table represents standardized z-scores. A z-score is written as: $z = \frac{X-\mu}{\sigma}$, where X represents the particular value, μ represents the population mean, and σ represents the population standard deviation. (Literally translated, a z-score represents the number of standard deviations a value is above, or below, the mean.)For instance, if we wanted to find the area under the curve between 105 and 115 for a normal distribution with a mean of 100 and a standard deviation of 10, we would first convert our values to those appropriate for a normal distribution, $\frac{105-100}{10} = 0.5$ and $\frac{115-100}{10} = 1.5$, and then look up 1.5 and 0.5 in the table and subtract the results.

Two-way frequency table

A two-way frequency table is a table that shows the number of data points falling into each combination of two categories in the form of a table, with one category on each axis. Creating a two-way frequency table is simply a matter of drawing a table with each axis labeled with the possibilities for the corresponding category, and then filling in the numbers in the appropriate cells. For instance, suppose you're told that at a given school, 30 male students take Spanish, 20 take French, and 25 German, while 26 female students take Spanish, 28 French, and 21 German. These data can be represented by the following two-way frequency table:

# of students	SPANISH	FRENCH	GERMAN
MALE	30	20	25
FEMALE	26	28	21

Joint and marginal frequencies

The joint frequency, P(X, Y), is the probability of belonging to two specific subcategories. It's also known as a joint probability or joint relative frequency. The marginal frequency,P(X), is the probability of belonging in a specific subcategory. It's also known as a marginal probability or marginal relative frequency. For example,

		Category #1 (Color)			TOTALS
		yellow	grey	black	
Category #2 (Vehicle)	truck	2	5	20	27
	car	2	25	3	30
	motorcycle	15	4	3	22
TOTALS		19	34	26	79

The joint frequency that a vehicle is a yellow truck is equal to $\frac{2}{79}$, where 2 is the number in the table cell corresponding to both "truck" and "yellow" and 79 is the total number of all vehicles of all colors.

The marginal frequency that a vehicle is a truck is equal to the sum of the probabilities of its being a yellow truck, a grey truck, or a black truck, $P(truck) = \frac{2}{79} + \frac{5}{79} + \frac{20}{79} = \frac{27}{79}$.

Conditional frequency

The conditional frequency, P(X|Y), is the probability that X is a certain value on the condition that Y is a certain value. It's also known as a conditional probability or conditional relative frequency. The conditional frequency is related to the joint frequency and the marginal frequency by the relation $P(X, Y) = P(X|Y)P(Y)$; thus knowing the joint and marginal frequencies we can find the conditional frequency.

For example, consider the following two-way frequency table .

		Category #1 (Color)			TOTALS
		yellow	grey	black	
Category #2 (Vehicle)	truck	2	5	20	27
	car	2	25	3	30
	motorcycle	15	4	3	22
TOTALS		19	34	26	79

The joint frequency that a vehicle is a yellow truck is equal to $\frac{2}{79}$, and the marginal frequency that a vehicle is a truck is $\frac{27}{79}$. Therefore, the conditional frequency that a vehicle is yellow on the condition that it is a truck (the probability that a given truck in the data set is yellow) is equal to $\frac{2}{79} \div \frac{27}{79} = \frac{2}{27}$.

Data on two quantitative variables on a scatter plot

Data sets on two quantitative variables can be represented on a scatter plot by plotting each data point as a separate point on the chart. One axis of the chart corresponds to each variable, and then the data points are plotted accordingly in the appropriate positions on each axis. For instance, if 50 widgets cost $500, 100 widgets cost $800, and 200 widgets cost $1500, this can be plotted on a scatter plot as follows:

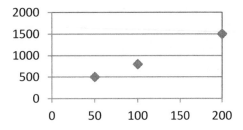

Normally, of course, a scatter plot would be used for larger data sets than this. A scatter plot is useful for seeing the relationship between the variables; one can often see at a glance if the variables have a linear or other simple relationship.

Identifying a function from a scatter plot of data of two variables

It's often possible from examining a scatter plot to see roughly what relationship exists between the data by estimating what kind of smooth curve would best fit the data points. Linear relationships are particularly easy to spot—do the data points look like they're roughly arranged in a straight line?—but other functions may also fit the data. Actually finding the parameters of the function for the most precise fit is a more complex matter, though most calculators and spreadsheets have the capability of performing the necessary calculations. Qualitatively judging what kind of function fits the data, however, is simpler. Below are examples of scatter plots fit to quadratic and exponential functions, respectively:

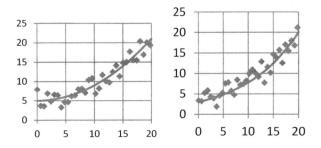

Using a function fitted to a scatter plot to solve problems

Linear functions

Once you have a function fitted to the scatter plot, you can use the equation of that function to solve problems regarding the data. For instance, suppose the scatter plot on the left below represents the number of bacteria that grow in a petri dish after one week, in millions, versus the amount of a certain nutrient added, in milligrams. The graph on the right shows a linear function fitted to the data.

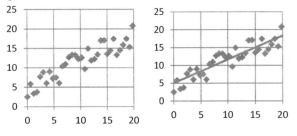

- 24 -

The equation of the line of best fit is $y = \frac{2}{3}x + 5$, where y is the bacteria count in millions and x is the amount of nutrient added, in milligrams. We can then use this function to solve problems; for instance, if we want to estimate how many bacteria to expect if we add 30 milligrams of nutrient, we solve $y = \frac{2}{3}(30) + 5 = 25$, or about 25 million bacteria.

Quadratic functions

Once you have a function fitted to the scatter plot, you can use the equation of that function to solve problems regarding the data. For instance, suppose the scatter plot on the left below represents the area covered by a certain patch of mold, in square centimeters, versus the time in days. The graph on the right shows a quadratic function fitted to the data.

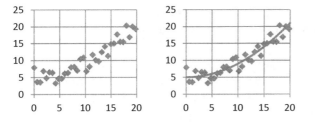

The equation of the quadratic trendline is $y = \frac{1}{25}x^2 + 5$, where x is the time in days and y is the area in square centimeters. We can then use this function to solve problems; for instance, if we want to estimate how much area to expect the mold to cover after 30 days, we solve $y = \frac{1}{25}(30^2) + 5 = 41$, or 41 square centimeters.

Exponential functions

Once you have a function fitted to the scatter plot, you can use the equation of that function to solve problems regarding the data. For instance, suppose the scatter plot on the left below represents the total assets of a certain company in millions of dollars, versus the time in years since 1990. The graph on the right shows an exponential function fitted to the data.

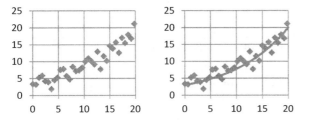

The equation of the trendline is $y = 3e^{0.095t}$, where t is the time in years and y is the company's assets, in millions of dollars. We can then use this function to solve problems; for instance, if we want to estimate the company's projected assets in the year 2020 (30 years after 1990), we solve $y = 3e^{0.095 \cdot 30} \approx 51.9$, or 51.9 million dollars.

Residuals of a fit to a data set

The residuals of a fit to a data set are the differences between the observed values of the data and the predicted values based on the fit. For example, consider the data set {(6,6), (8,12), (10,20), (12,30)}, shown in the scatter plot on the left below A linear fit to the graph is shown on the right:

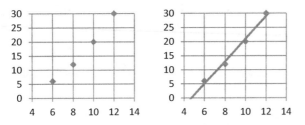

The line of best fit has the equation $y = 4x - 19$. The predicted value for $x = 6$ is then $4(6) - 19 = 5$, and the residual at $x = 6$ is $6 - 5 = 1$. At $x = 8$, the predicted value is $4(8) - 19 = 13$, and the residual at $x = 8$ is $12 - 13 = -1$. Similarly, the residuals at $x = 10$ and $x = 12$ are -1 and 1, respectively.

Note that these residuals add to 0 $(1 + (-1) + (-1) + 1 = 0)$. For the best fit curve, this is always the case; the sum and mean of the residuals will always be zero.

Residual plot

A residual plot is simply the plot of the residuals of a fit to a data set versus the independent variable (the x coordinates of the points). If the residual plot looks random—if the residuals seem to bear no relation to the independent variable—then the function fit to the model was probably a good choice. If the residual plot shows a definite pattern, then the data is probably better suited to a different kind of curve. Consider, for instance, the two residual plots shown below, both corresponding to linear fits. The plot on the left shows no obvious pattern, indicating that the linear fit in question is appropriate to the data. The plot on the left, however, shows a pronounced U shape, indicating that a nonlinear function would be a better fit to the data.

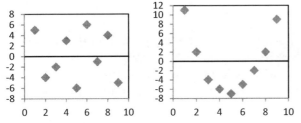

Estimating a fit to a linear function without the aid of technology

Although it's complicated to calculate an exact fit to a linear function without the aid of technology, finding an approximate fit is feasible. To produce such a fit, first draw a line that seems to follow the data points as closely as possible, probably with about as many data points above the line as below it. Then find the equation for this linear fit the same way as you would find the equation of any graphed line: choose two points on the line, (x_1, y_1) and (x_2, y_2), and then find the slope of the line as $m = \frac{y_2 - y_1}{x_2 - x_1}$. Then use this value of m and one of the known points in the equation $y = mx + b$ to solve for b (it doesn't matter which of the two points you use).

Because this method involves some eyeballing and approximation, it will generally not be completely optimal, and two people may get slightly different results. However, this approximate result will typically be good enough to find estimated solutions to problems.

Finding a fit to a linear function using technology

Most modern calculators and spreadsheets have the functionality to calculate linear fits to data sets. On a TI-84, you can find the fit as follows: First, press "STAT", select "EDIT", and enter your data into the table, with the independent variable in the L1 column and the dependent in the L2. Then press "STAT" again, select "CALC", and select "LinReg(ax+b)". The screen will display the coefficients a and b of the linear fit. In recent versions of Microsoft Excel, you can put the independent and dependent variables in adjacent columns, select all the data, and insert a scatter plot. Then right-click on one of the data points of the graph and select "Add Trendline". Select "Linear", and be sure to check "Display Equation on chart" before clicking OK. The linear plot should be displayed on the graph, along with the corresponding equation of the line.

Slope of a linear model

In the case of a linear fit to a data set, of the form $y = mx + b$, the slope m corresponds to the rate of change of the dependent variable y with respect to the independent variable x. This can often be expressed in a form similar to "y per x". For instance, if the data represents the distance of an object from some point as a function of time, with the distance as y and the time as x, then the slope of the linear model represents the change in distance with respect to the corresponding change in time—i.e., the velocity. If the data represents the cost to produce various quantities of products, then the slope of the linear model is the change in the cost with respect to the quantity of products produced—i.e., the production cost per unit of product.

Intercept of a linear model

In the case of a linear fit to a data set, of the form $y = mx + b$, the intercept b corresponds to the value of the dependent variable y when the independent variable x is equal to zero. This often can be expressed as the "initial value" of the variable, or as its offset. For instance, if the data represents the distance of an object from some point as a function of time, with the distance as y and the time as x, then the intercept of the linear model represents the object's distance at time zero—i.e., its initial distance. If the data represents the cost to produce various quantities of products, then the intercept of the linear model is the cost when no units are being produced—in other words, the overhead cost involved in the production.

Correlation coefficient of a linear fit

The correlation coefficient of a linear fit is a number that expresses how closely the linear fit approximates the function. The coefficient is negative if the line of best fit has a negative slope—the dependent variable decreases as the independent variable increases, and positive if the best fit has a positive slope—the dependent variable increases as the independent variable increases. The linear fit is most closely correlated to the data if the correlation coefficient is equal to ± 1; this means that all the data points lie exactly on the best fit line. If the correlation coefficient is equal to 0, then the data are completely uncorrelated; there is no relationship between the dependent and the independent variable. More often, the correlation coefficient is somewhere in between 0 and 1, indicating a fit that reveals some correlation between the variables.

<u>Computation using technology</u>
Most modern calculators and spreadsheets have the functionality to calculate the correlation coefficients of linear fits to data sets. On a TI-84, you can find the fit as follows: First, press "STAT", select "EDIT", and enter your data into the table, with the independent variable in the L1 column and the dependent in the L2. Then press "STAT" again, select "CALC", and select "LinReg(ax+b)". In addition to the coefficients a and b of the linear fit, the screen will display the correlation coefficient, r. In recent versions of Microsoft Excel, you can put the independent and dependent variables in adjacent columns, then in another cell type "=CORREL(". Select the cells containing the independent variables, then type a comma, select the cells containing the dependent variables and type a closing parenthesis. The cell should contain something like "=CORREL(A1:A10,B1:B10)", though the letters and numbers may differ. Press ENTER, and the cell will show the correlation coefficient of a linear fit to the data.

Two correlated variables

Two variables are correlated if some nonrandom relationship exists between them: if a change in one variable tends to correspond to a change in the other. While many relationships may exist between variables—they may have a quadratic relationship, or an exponential, for example—"correlation" often refers to linear correlation, the existence of a linear relationship $y = mx + b$ between the variables. The data points need not perfectly follow that line; if they do, they are perfectly correlated, but data that approximately follow close to a line may still be said to be correlated. The degree of correlation may be quantified by a value called the correlation coefficient.
Note that correlation is not the same thing as causation; just because two variables are correlated does not necessarily mean that one is the cause of the other.

Correlation and causation

Two variables are correlated if a change in one variable is accompanied by a change in the other, especially if the two variables have a linear relationship. Causation exists if one variable directly depends on the other; a change in one variable causes a change in the other. Note that correlation does not imply causation. If two variables x and y are correlated, it could be because x causes y. However, it could also be that the apparent correlation is coincidental, or that y causes x, or it could be that both x and y are influenced by a third variable separate from both x and y.

Two variables correlated but not linked by causation

Many examples could be constructed of data sets with variables that are correlated but in which one variable is not the cause of the other. One way to construct such a data set is to consider two variables that might both be affected by a third. For example, suppose a survey at a given school indicates that students' shoe sizes are correlated with their spelling; the students with larger shoe sizes tend to have better spelling. Clearly it would seem strange that larger feet would lead to better spelling. In fact, there's a third variable at play here: older students would tend to have larger feet, and likewise older students will tend to have better spelling. The larger shoe sizes don't cause the better spelling, nor does the better spelling cause the larger shoe sizes; rather, both are caused by a third variable that wasn't measured.

Geometry

Tangent

<u>Example problem</u>
If the sine of an acute angle is 0.4, what is the angle's tangent? Give an exact answer.

Imagine the angle is an angle in a right triangle. The sine is the ratio of the opposite leg to the hypotenuse; if the sine is 0.4, then the leg is 0.4 times the length of the hypotenuse. Let's say the leg is 2 units long and the hypotenuse is 5 units (we can choose any lengths we want, because in any similar triangle the ratios will still be the same). By the Pythagorean theorem, the other leg is $\sqrt{21}$ units. The tangent is the ratio of the opposite leg to the adjacent leg, so it is $\frac{2}{\sqrt{21}}$; rationalizing the denominator gives us a final answer of $\frac{2\sqrt{21}}{21}$.

Trigonometric ratio sine

<u>Example problem</u>
Define the trigonometric ratio sine for an acute angle using ratios of sides in similar right triangles.

Similar triangles have three pairs of congruent angles and three pairs of proportional sides. The proportion has the same value for all pairs of sides, so $\frac{a}{d} = \frac{c}{f}$ or (using cross multiplication and division to reorganize) $\frac{a}{c} = \frac{d}{f}$. The trigonometric ratio sine is opposite over hypotenuse. In $\triangle ABC$, $\sin A = \frac{a}{c}$ and in $\triangle DEF$, $\sin D = \frac{d}{f}$. So since $\frac{a}{c} = \frac{d}{f}$, $\sin A = \sin D$. This shows that the trigonometric ratio sine is a property of the angle because the ratio is the same in both triangles even though the triangles are different sizes.

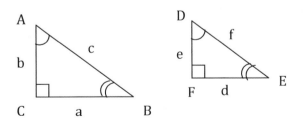

Trigonometric ratio cosine

<u>Example problem</u>
Define the trigonometric ratio cosine for an acute angle using ratios of sides in similar right triangles.

Similar triangles have three pairs of congruent angles and three pairs of proportional sides. The proportion has the same value for all pairs of sides, so $\frac{b}{e} = \frac{c}{f}$ or (using cross multiplication and division to reorganize) $\frac{b}{c} = \frac{e}{f}$. The trigonometric ratio cosine is adjacent over hypotenuse. In $\triangle ABC$, $\cos A = \frac{b}{c}$ and in $\triangle DEF$, $\cos D = \frac{e}{f}$. So since $\frac{b}{c} = \frac{e}{f}$, $\cos A = \cos D$. This shows that the trigonometric ratio cosine is a property of the angle because the ratio is the same in both triangles even though the triangles are different sizes.

Trigonometric ratio tangent

<u>Example problem</u>
Define the trigonometric ratio tangent for an acute angle using ratios of sides in similar right triangles.

Similar triangles have three pairs of congruent angles and three pairs of proportional sides. The proportion has the same value for all pairs of sides, so $\frac{a}{d} = \frac{b}{e}$ or (using cross multiplication and division to reorganize) $\frac{a}{b} = \frac{d}{e}$. The trigonometric ratio tangent is opposite over adjacent. In $\triangle ABC$, $\tan A = \frac{a}{b}$ and in $\triangle DEF$, $\tan D = \frac{d}{e}$. So since $\frac{a}{b} = \frac{d}{e}$, $\tan A = \tan D$. This shows that the trigonometric ratio tangent is a property of the angle because the ratio is the same in both triangles even though the triangles are different sizes.

Sine and cosine of complementary angles

The sum of two complementary angles is 90°. In a right triangle, the two acute angles are complementary because the sum of the angles (180°) minus the right angle (90°) leaves the sum of the acute angles (90°). So, $m\angle A + m\angle B = 90°$. $\sin A = \frac{opp}{hyp} = \frac{a}{c}$ and $\cos B = \frac{adj}{hyp} = \frac{a}{c}$, thus the sine of an angle is equal to the cosine of its complementary angle.

Problems solved using sine

Problems that can be solved using sine must give specific information and ask for a specific solution.

Given:	Unknown:
one acute angle and the side opposite that angle	the hypotenuse
one acute angle and the hypotenuse	the side opposite that angle
the hypotenuse and one leg	the angle opposite the known leg **to solve this problem, use $\sin^{-1}$**

Law of Sines

The Law of Sines states that for any $\triangle ABC$, $\frac{\sin A}{a} = \frac{\sin B}{b} = \frac{\sin C}{c}$. To prove this, draw an auxiliary line from the vertex at B, perpendicular to AC. Notice that $\sin A = \frac{h}{c}$, so $\frac{\sin A}{a} = \frac{\frac{h}{c}}{a} = \frac{h}{c} \cdot \frac{1}{a} = \frac{h}{a \cdot c}$. Notice that $\sin C = \frac{h}{a}$, so $\frac{\sin C}{c} = \frac{\frac{h}{a}}{c} = \frac{h}{a} \cdot \frac{1}{c} = \frac{h}{a \cdot c}$. Therefore, $\frac{\sin A}{a} = \frac{\sin C}{c}$.

Now, draw an auxiliary line (call it g) from another vertex C) perpendicular to the opposite side AB to create two other right triangles. Notice that $\sin A = \frac{g}{b}$, so $\frac{\sin A}{a} = \frac{\frac{g}{b}}{a} = \frac{g}{b} \cdot \frac{1}{a} = \frac{g}{a \cdot b}$.

Notice that $\sin B = \frac{g}{a}$, so $\frac{\sin B}{b} = \frac{\frac{g}{a}}{b} = \frac{g}{a} \cdot \frac{1}{b} = \frac{g}{a \cdot b}$. Therefore, $\frac{\sin A}{a} = \frac{\sin B}{b}$. Since $\frac{\sin A}{a} = \frac{\sin C}{c}$ and $\frac{\sin A}{a} = \frac{\sin B}{b}$ are both true, $\frac{\sin A}{a} = \frac{\sin B}{b} = \frac{\sin C}{c}$ is also true.

Problems that can be solved using the Law of Sines must give specific information and ask for a specific solution.

Given:	Unknown:
two sides and an angle opposite one side	the angle opposite the other side
two angles and a side (find the third angle using the Angle Sum Theorem if necessary)	the side opposite any angle

<u>Example problems</u>
Problem 1: Given $\triangle ABC$ and $\triangle DEF$,
Find the measure of $\angle C$.
Find the measure of $\angle A$.
Find the length of BC.

$\frac{\sin C}{AB} = \frac{\sin B}{AC} \rightarrow \frac{\sin C}{7.5} = \frac{\sin 63}{10} \rightarrow \sin C = \frac{7.5 \cdot \sin 63}{10} = 0.668 \rightarrow C =$ $\sin^{-1} 0.668 = 41.9°$.

Since the sum of the angles in a triangle is $180°$, $m\angle A = 180 - (63 + 41.9 = 180 - 104.9 = 75.1°$.

$\frac{\sin A}{BC} = \frac{\sin B}{AC} \rightarrow \frac{\sin 75.1}{BC} = \frac{\sin 63}{10} \rightarrow BC \cdot \sin 63 = 10 \cdot \sin 75.1 \rightarrow BC = \frac{10 \cdot \sin 75.1}{\sin 63} = 10.85$.

Problem 2: Given $\triangle ABC$ and $\triangle DEF$,
Find the measure of $\angle E$.
Find the length of DE.
Find the length of DF.

Since the sum of the angles in a triangle is $180°$, $m\angle E = 180 - (72 + 74) = 180 - 146 = 34°$.

$\frac{\sin F}{DE} = \frac{\sin D}{EF} \rightarrow \frac{\sin 74}{DE} = \frac{\sin 72}{15} \rightarrow DE \cdot \sin 72 = 15 \cdot \sin 74 \rightarrow DE = \frac{15 \cdot \sin 74}{\sin 72} = 15.16$.

$\frac{\sin E}{DF} = \frac{\sin D}{EF} \rightarrow \frac{\sin 34}{DF} = \frac{\sin 72}{15} \rightarrow DF \cdot \sin 72 = 15 \cdot \sin 34 \rightarrow DF = \frac{15 \cdot \sin 34}{\sin 72} = 8.82$.

Problem 3: Use the Law of Sines and the illustration to solve the following problem:
Bob is camping near a river. Bob walks upstream and finds a place to cross the river (point
A). Then he turns and walks along stream for 40 feet until he is past the camp and at
another river crossing (point *B*). How far is Bob from the tent at each crossing?

The Law of Sines is used to solve for an unknown side when two angles and
one of the sides opposite an angle are known. In this problem, it is possible
to find the third angle, which is opposite the known side, and use it to solve
for the two missing side lengths.

$m\angle tent = 180 - (23 + 17) = 180 - 40 = 140°$.

$\frac{\sin tent}{AB} = \frac{\sin B}{b} \rightarrow \frac{\sin 140}{40} = \frac{\sin 23}{b} \rightarrow b \cdot \sin 140 = 40 \cdot \sin 23 \rightarrow b = \frac{40 \cdot \sin 23}{\sin 140} =$
23.31. The distance from the tent to the first crossing is 23.31 feet.

$\frac{\sin tent}{AB} = \frac{\sin A}{a} \rightarrow \frac{\sin 140}{40} = \frac{\sin 17}{a} \rightarrow a \cdot \sin 140 = 40 \cdot \sin 17 \rightarrow a = \frac{40 \cdot \sin 17}{\sin 140} =$
18.19. The distance from the second crossing to the tent is 18.19 feet.

Problem 4: Use the Law of Sines to solve the following problem:
Seth is building a tree house in a 15-foot tree on a hill in his backyard. At the base of the tree
are rosebushes, which his mother will not let him remove. Seth has decided to build a 23.7-
foot ladder from the base of the hill to the top of the tree. If the tree meets the ground at a
115° angle, at what angle will the ladder meet the hill?

The Law of Sines is used to solve for an angle when another angle and the
two sides opposite those angles are known.

$\frac{\sin L}{l} = \frac{\sin T}{t} \rightarrow \frac{\sin 115}{23.7} = \frac{\sin T}{15} \rightarrow 23.7 \cdot \sin T = 15 \cdot \sin 115 \rightarrow \sin T =$
$\frac{15 \cdot \sin 115}{23.7} = 0.574 \rightarrow T = \sin^{-1} 0.574 = 35°$. The ladder will meet the hill at
an angle of 35°.

Law of Cosines

The Law of Cosines states: $c^2 = a^2 + b^2 - 2 \cdot a \cdot b \cdot \cos C$. To prove this, draw an auxiliary
line from the vertex at *B*, perpendicular to *AC*. Side *b* is now split into two lengths, *x* and
$b - x$.

use the Pythagorean Theorem to write an equation about the right triangle with hypotenuse *a*	$a^2 = x^2 + h^2$
use trigonometry to write a cosine equation about angle *C*	$\cos C = \frac{x}{a}$ $x = a \cdot \cos C$
use the Pythagorean Theorem two write an equation about the right triangle with hypotenuse *c*	$c^2 = (b - x)^2 + h^2$ $c^2 = (b^2 - 2 \cdot b \cdot x + x^2) + h^2$ $c^2 = b^2 - 2 \cdot b \cdot x + (x^2 + h^2)$
substitute a^2 for $(x^2 + h^2)$	$c^2 = b^2 - 2 \cdot b \cdot x + a^2$ $c^2 = a^2 + b^2 - 2 \cdot b \cdot x$
substitute $a \cdot \cos C$ for *x*	$c^2 = a^2 + b^2 - 2 \cdot b \cdot (a \cdot \cos C)$ $c^2 = a^2 + b^2 - 2 \cdot a \cdot b \cdot \cos C$

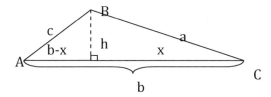

Problems that can be solved using the Law of Cosines must give specific information and ask for a specific solution.

Given:	Unknown:	Form of the Equation:
two sides and the angle between them	the third side	$c^2 = a^2 + b^2 - 2 \cdot a \cdot b \cdot \cos C$
three sides	any angle	$\cos C = \dfrac{a^2 + b^2 - c^2}{2 \cdot a \cdot b}$

Example problems
Problem 1: Given $\triangle ABC$, use the Law of Cosines to
Find the length of BC.
Find the measure of $\angle B$.
Find the measure of $\angle C$.

$$BC^2 = AB^2 + AC^2 - 2 \cdot AB \cdot AC \cdot \cos A = (29.41)^2 + (17.5)^2 - 2 \cdot (29.41) \cdot (17.5) \cdot \cos 36 = 338.436 \rightarrow BC = \sqrt{338.436} = 18.40.$$

$\cos B = \dfrac{AB^2 + BC^2 - AC^2}{2 \cdot AB \cdot BC} = \dfrac{29.41^2 + 18.4^2 - 17.5^2}{2 \cdot 29.41 \cdot 18.4} = 0.829 \rightarrow B = \cos^{-1} 0.829 = 34°.$

$\cos C = \dfrac{BC^2 + AC^2 - AB^2}{2 \cdot BC \cdot AC} = \dfrac{18.4^2 + 17.5^2 - 29.41^2}{2 \cdot 18.4 \cdot 17.5} = -0.342 \rightarrow C = \cos^{-1} -0.342 = 110°.$

Problem 2: Given $\triangle DEF$, use the Law of Cosines to
Find the measure of $\angle D$.
Find the measure of $\angle E$.
Find the measure of $\angle F$.

$\cos D = \dfrac{DE^2 + DF^2 - EF^2}{2 \cdot DE \cdot DF} = \dfrac{8.78^2 + 10.88^2 - 13^2}{2 \cdot 8.78 \cdot 10.88} = 0.139 \rightarrow D = \cos^{-1} 0.139 = 82.04°.$

$\cos E = \dfrac{DE^2 + EF^2 - DF^2}{2 \cdot DE \cdot EF} = \dfrac{8.78^2 + 13^2 - 10.88^2}{2 \cdot 8.78 \cdot 13} = 0.559 \rightarrow E = \cos^{-1} 0.559 = 55.98°.$

$\cos F = \dfrac{DF^2 + EF^2 - DE^2}{2 \cdot DF \cdot EF} = \dfrac{10.88^2 + 13^2 - 8.78^2}{2 \cdot 10.88 \cdot 13} = 0.743 \rightarrow F = \cos^{-1} 0.743 = 41.98°.$

Problem 3: Use the Law of Cosines to solve the following problem:
Sally is flying her plane on the heading shown in the figure. The plane's instrument panel indicates an air speed of 140 mph. However, there is a crosswind of 53 mph. What is the apparent speed (x) of the plane to an observer on the ground?

The Law of Cosines is used to solve for the third side in a triangle when two sides and the angle between them are known.
$$x^2 = (53)^2 + (140)^2 - 2 \cdot 53 \cdot 140 \cdot \cos 50 = 12870.03 \rightarrow x = \sqrt{12870.03} = 113.45 \text{mph}.$$

Problem 4: Use the Law of Cosines to solve the following problem:
Beth is returning to her campsite from an ATV ride when she remembers she still has to pay for the campsite. Earlier, she entered the locations of her campsite and the ranger station into her GPS. The GPS tells her that she is 5 miles from her tent and 8 miles from the ranger station. If Beth also knows that her tent is 4 miles from the ranger station, how many degrees must she alter her course to pay the bill before returning to her campsite?

The Law of Cosines is used to solve for an angle in a triangle when three sides are known. Begin by drawing a picture and assigning letters to the three locations: A for ATV, C for Campsite, and R for Ranger Station. Applying the law of cosines to our triangle gives us $CR^2 = AC^2 + AR^2 - 2 \cdot AC \cdot AR \cdot \cos A$. Since we're looking for angle A, we can rearrange the equation: $\cos A = \frac{AR^2 + AC^2 - CR^2}{2 \cdot AR \cdot AC} = \frac{8^2 + 5^2 - 4^2}{2 \cdot 8 \cdot 5} = 0.9125 \rightarrow A = \cos^{-1} 0.9125 = 24.15°$. Beth must alter her course by 24.15° to head toward the ranger station.

Trigometric ratios of right triangles

The six basic trigonometric ratios of right triangles are defined below:

$$\sin A = \frac{\text{opposite side}}{\text{hypotenuse}} = \frac{a}{c} \qquad \csc A = \frac{\text{hypotenuse}}{\text{opposite side}} = \frac{c}{a}$$

$$\cos A = \frac{\text{adjacent side}}{\text{hypotenuse}} = \frac{b}{c} \qquad \sec A = \frac{\text{hypotenuse}}{\text{adjacent side}} = \frac{c}{b}$$

$$\tan A = \frac{\text{opposite side}}{\text{adjacent side}} = \frac{a}{b} \qquad \cot A = \frac{\text{adjacent side}}{\text{opposite side}} = \frac{b}{a}$$

In the diagram below, angle C is the right angle, and side c is the hypotenuse. Side a is the side adjacent to angle B and side b is the side adjacent to angle A. These formulas will work for any acute angle in a right triangle. They will NOT work for any triangle that is not a right triangle. Also, they will not work for the right angle in a right triangle, since there is not a distinct adjacent side to differentiate from the hypotenuse.

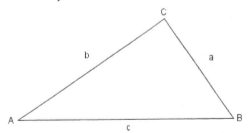

Intersection of a plane with a cylinder

When a plane intersects a cylinder at right angles to the cylinder's axis, the intersection is a circle.
When a plane intersects a cylinder at a skew angle to the cylinder's axis, the intersection is an ellipse. (If the cylinder is finitely long, the ellipse may be cut off if the plane also intersects one or both ends of the cylinder. In that case, it is a truncated ellipse, cut off at

one or both ends by lines that are perpendicular to its major axis.) When a plane intersects a cylinder parallel to the cylinder's axis, the intersection is a rectangle. (The rectangle is as long as the cylinder if the cylinder is finitely long, and is infinitely long if the cylinder is infinitely long. The rectangle's width depends on where the plane intersects the cylinder; it equals the cylinder's width if the plane passes down the cylinder's middle, and equals zero (in other words, the rectangle is just a line) if the plane is tangent to the cylinder.)

Nets

Example problems
Problem 1: Which of the following nets can and cannot be used to form a prism?

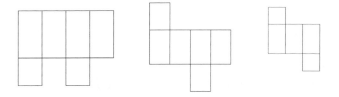

None of the nets shown can be used to form a prism.
In the first net, the "end" squares are both on the same side. Folding the net would result in one end of the prism being doubled over and the other end being empty. In the second net, the side lengths of the end faces do not match the lengths of the faces that would be joined to them. In the third net, there are simply not enough faces. A square prism needs six faces, and this net has only five.

Problem 2: Which of the following nets can and cannot be used to form a pyramid?

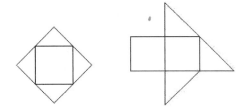

Only one of the nets shown can be used to form a pyramid. The first net has the right number of faces, but the faces are not large enough. The areas of the four triangular faces add up to that of the square face, so folding them inward would just create another flat square; two flat squares are not enough to make a solid. The second net has two square faces; a pyramid cannot have more than one non-triangular face. The third net has four triangular faces, which will form a pyramid with a triangular base.

Ellipse that is taller than wide

An ellipse is the set of all points in a plane, whose total distance from two fixed points called the foci (singular: focus) is constant, and whose center is the midpoint between the foci.

The standard equation of an ellipse that is taller than it is wide is $\frac{(y-k)^2}{a^2} + \frac{(x-h)^2}{b^2} = 1$, where a and b are coefficients. The center is the point (h, k) and the foci are the points $(h, k + c)$ and $(h, k - c)$, where $c^2 = a^2 - b^2$ and $a^2 > b^2$.

- 35 -

The major axis has length $2a$, and the minor axis has length $2b$.
Eccentricity (e) is a measure of how elongated an ellipse is, and is the ratio of the distance between the foci to the length of the major axis. Eccentricity will have a value between 0 and 1. The closer to 1 the eccentricity is, the closer the ellipse is to being a circle. The formula for eccentricity is $= \frac{c}{a}$.

Ellipse that is wider than tall

An ellipse is the set of all points in a plane, whose total distance from two fixed points called the foci (singular: focus) is constant, and whose center is the midpoint between the foci. The standard equation of an ellipse that is wider than it is tall is
$\frac{(x-h)^2}{a^2} + \frac{(y-k)^2}{b^2} = 1$, where a and b are coefficients. The center is the point (h, k) and the foci are the points $(h + c, k)$ and $(h - c, k)$, where $c^2 = a^2 - b^2$ and $a^2 > b^2$.
The major axis has length $2a$, and the minor axis has length $2b$.
Eccentricity (e) is a measure of how elongated an ellipse is, and is the ratio of the distance between the foci to the length of the major axis. Eccentricity will have a value between 0 and 1. The closer to 1 the eccentricity is, the closer the ellipse is to being a circle. The formula for eccentricity is $= \frac{c}{a}$.

Parabola

A parabola is the set of all points in a plane that are equidistant from a fixed line, called the directrix, and a fixed point not on the line, called the focus.
Axis: The line perpendicular to the directrix that passes through the focus.
For parabolas that open up or down, the standard equation is
$(x - h)^2 = 4c(y - k)$, where h, c, and k are coefficients. If c is positive, the parabola opens up. If c is negative, the parabola opens down. The vertex is the point (h, k). The directrix is the line having the equation $y = -c + k$, and the focus is the point $(h, c + k)$.
For parabolas that open left or right, the standard equation is
$(y - k)^2 = 4c(x - h)$, where k, c, and h are coefficients. If c is positive, the parabola opens to the right. If c is negative, the parabola opens to the left. The vertex is the point (h, k). The directrix is the line having the equation
$x = -c + h$, and the focus is the point $(c + h, k)$.

Horizontal hyperbola

A hyperbola is the set of all points in a plane, whose distance from two fixed points, called foci, has a constant difference.

The standard equation of a horizontal hyperbola is $\frac{(x-h)^2}{a^2} - \frac{(y-k)^2}{b^2} = 1$, where a, b, h, and k are real numbers. The center is the point (h, k), the vertices are the points $(h + a, k)$ and $(h - a, k)$, and the foci are the points that every point on one of the parabolic curves is equidistant from and are found using the formulas $(h + c, k)$ and $(h - c, k)$, where $c^2 = a^2 + b^2$. The asymptotes are two lines the graph of the hyperbola approaches but never reaches, and are given by the equations $y = \left(\frac{b}{a}\right)(x - h) + k$ and $y = -\left(\frac{b}{a}\right)(x - h) + k$.

Vertical hyperbola

A vertical hyperbola is formed when a plane makes a vertical cut through two cones that are stacked vertex-to-vertex. The standard equation of a vertical hyperbola is $\frac{(y-k)^2}{a^2} - \frac{(x-h)^2}{b^2} = 1$, where a, b, k, and h are real numbers. The center is the point (h, k), the vertices are the points $(h, k + a)$ and $(h, k - a)$, and the foci are the points that every point on one of the parabolic curves is equidistant from and are found using the formulas $(h, k + c)$ and $(h, k - c)$, where $c^2 = a^2 + b^2$. The asymptotes are two lines the graph of the hyperbola approaches but never reach, and are given by the equations $y = \left(\frac{a}{b}\right)(x - h) + k$ and $y = -\left(\frac{a}{b}\right)(x - h) + k$.

Transformations

The four basic transformations are translation, rotation, reflection, and dilation. In a transformation, all the points in the figure are moved the same distance in the same linear direction. In a rotation, all the points in the figure are rotated the same distance about a center point. (This center point is not necessarily the center of the figure.) In a reflection, all the points in the figure are reflected across the same line. (This line may or may not pass through the figure itself.) In a dilation, all the points in the figure are moved an equal (that is, proportional) distance toward or away from the center; in other words, the figure grows or shrinks while keeping the same shape.

When all the points on a plane are translated the same linear distance, none of them stay in their original locations (unless the distance is zero, in which case all of them do).

When the points on a plane are rotated by an angle about a point P, only P stays where it is (unless the angle is zero, in which case all the points are preserved).

When the points on a plane are reflected across a line l, only the points on line l are preserved.

When a plane is stretched so that all the points move toward or away from center point C by the same factor, only point C is preserved (again, unless the dilation is by a factor of 1, in which case all the points are preserved).

Combination of transformations

Any two different transformations can be combined: a translation with a rotation, reflection, or dilation; a rotation with a reflection or dilation; or a reflection with a dilation. Also, a reflection can be combined with another reflection about a different axis, a rotation can be combined with another rotation about a different point, and a dilation can be combined with another dilation with a different center. (A translation combined with another translation, however, is just the same as a single translation; for example, a translation two units left and one unit down combined with a translation one unit left and two units up is just the same as a single translation three units left and one unit up.)

All single plane transformations except dilations preserve the size of the original figure; hence any combination of transformations that does not include a dilation will also preserve the figure's size.

Incenter, circumcenter, orthocenter, and centroid of a triangle

The incenter is the point where the bisectors of the triangle's interior angles meet. The circumcenter is the point where the perpendicular bisectors of the triangle's sides meet. The orthocenter is the point where the triangle's altitudes—the perpendicular lines from each vertex to the opposite side—all meet. The centroid is the point where the triangle's medians—the lines connecting each vertex to the center of the opposite side—all meet. The centroid, circumcenter, and orthocenter are always collinear, and the line they lie on is called the Euler line. The incenter usually does not lie on the Euler line.

Distance and midpoint formulas

If the coordinates of points A and B are (x_1, y_1) and (x_2, y_2) respectively, then the formula for the distance between them is $D = \sqrt{(x_1 - x_2)^2 + (y_1 - y_2)^2}$. This is based on the Pythagorean theorem; the square of the diagonal distance between the points is the sum of the squares of the horizontal and vertical distances.

The midpoint of AB has the coordinates $(\frac{(x_1 - x_2)}{2}, \frac{(y_1 - y_2)}{2})$. In other words, its x-coordinate is halfway between the x-coordinates of A and B, and its y-coordinate is halfway between their y-coordinates.

To find the midpoint of segment AB, it isn't necessary to find the length or slope of AB. All that is necessary is to find the point that is midway between A and B in the x-direction and midway between them in the y-direction; then, by the properties of similar triangles, that point will also be midway between them on the line connecting them directly.

Determining types of quadrilaterals

Rectangle

Given the coordinates of points A, B, C, and D in a two-dimensional coordinate plane, for $ABCD$ to be a rectangle, it must have two pairs of parallel sides, which must be perpendicular to each other. The best way to determine this is by finding the slopes of all four sides: AB, BC, CD, and DA. If AB and CD have the same slope, they are parallel; if BC and DA have the same slope, they are also parallel. Finally, if AB and BC have slopes that are negative reciprocals of each other, they are perpendicular. If all these things are true, $ABCD$ is a rectangle; if any one of these things is not true, $ABCD$ is not a rectangle.

Kite

Given the coordinates of points A, B, C, and D in a two-dimensional coordinate plane, two methods will work equally to determine whether quadrilateral $ABCD$ is a kite. One method depends on the fact that a kite has two pairs of adjacent sides that are the same length, and the other method depends on the fact that a kite's diagonals are perpendicular and one of them bisects the other. To use the first method, use the distance formula to find the lengths of segments AB, BC, CD, and DA. If AB and BC are congruent and CD and DA are congruent, or if BC and CD are congruent and DA and AB are congruent, then $ABCD$ is a kite; otherwise it is not. To use the second method, first find the slopes of the diagonals AC and BD. If the slopes are negative reciprocals of each other, then the diagonals are perpendicular. Next, use the midpoint formula to find the midpoints, *E* and *F*, of *AC* and *BD* respectively. Then, use the distance formula to find out if *EB* and *ED* are the same length, or if *FA* and *FC* are the same length. If EB = ED or FA = FC, then *ABCD* is a kite; otherwise it is not.

Finding the radius of a circle

A circle in the coordinate plane has its center at (3, 1). One point on the circle is (6, -3). Given the center and one point on the circle, we can find the circle's radius using the distance formula based on the Pythagorean theorem. The horizontal distance between the two points is 6 – 3 = 3, and the vertical distance is 1 – (-3) = 4. Therefore, the straight-line distance between the points is $\sqrt{3^2 + 4^2}$, or 5 units. Since the radius of the circle is 5 units, any point in the plane that is 5 units from the center of the circle will be a point on the circle. To find another such point, we could go 3 units down and 4 units across, or 4 units up or down and 3 units across, to get a point like (7, 4). We could also simply go 5 units up, down, or across, to get a point like (-2, 1).

Finding the circumcenter of a triangle

The circumcenter is the point where the perpendicular bisectors of the sides intersect; finding the intersection of any two bisectors is sufficient. So, suppose we choose to find the bisectors of sides *AB* and *BC*. First we use the midpoint formula to find the midpoint of side *AB*. Then, we find the slope of *AB*, knowing that a line perpendicular to *AB* will have a slope that is the negative reciprocal of this. Now that we know the slope of the perpendicular bisector and also know that it must pass through the midpoint of *AB*, we can use the point-slope formula to find the equation of this line. Then we repeat for side *BC*, so we now have equations of both bisecting lines; finally, we solve the system of those two equations to find the point where they intersect. This point is the circumcenter of *ABC*.

Example problems

Problem 1
In a regular hexagon of side length 10, what is the perpendicular distance between two opposite sides?

If we divide a regular hexagon into six equilateral triangles, we can see that the height of each of those triangles is equal to $\sqrt{3}$ times half the length of the base, where the base of the triangle is also a side of the hexagon. The height of one of the equilateral triangles is also half the distance between opposite sides of the hexagon, so the distance between the sides of the hexagon is equal to $\sqrt{3}$ times the length of one side. Therefore, if the sides of the hexagon measure 10 units each, the distance between two opposite sides is $10\sqrt{3}$ units.

Problem 2

In a regular octagon, how many pairs of diagonals that are perpendicular to each other can be drawn?

Consider the regular octagon *ABCDEFGH*. First consider the diagonals that connect vertices that have three sides between them—*AF* and *BE*, for example. There are eight of these diagonals, each parallel to two sides and perpendicular to two more, and we can easily see that each one is perpendicular to exactly two others. Therefore, there are eight pairs of perpendicular diagonals in this set.

Next, consider the diagonals that connect vertices that have two sides between them, like *AC* and *CE*. There are eight of these, and each one is perpendicular to two others, so there are also eight perpendicular pairs of these diagonals.

Finally, consider the diagonals that connect opposite vertices, like *AE*. There are only four of these, and they come in two perpendicular pairs.

Since the above three types are the only kinds of diagonals possible, there are 18 pairs of perpendicular diagonals.

Problem 3

In a regular decagon (a 10-sided figure), how many pairs of diagonals that are parallel to each other can be drawn?

Consider the decagon *ABCDEFGHJK*. Sides *AB* and *FG* are parallel to each other, and there are also three diagonals that are parallel to both these sides: *CK, DJ,* and *EH*. The same is true for each pair of parallel sides. Since there are five pairs of parallel sides, there are therefore five such sets of three parallel diagonals. This includes all the diagonals that connect pairs of vertices that have an odd number of sides separating them.

Next, consider a diagonal that connects two vertices that have an even number of sides between them, such as *AC*. This diagonal is parallel to diagonals *DK, EJ,* and *FH,* and there are four more such sets of four parallel diagonals. These twenty diagonals plus the fifteen above include all thirty-five of the decagon's diagonals.

From each set of three parallel diagonals, three different parallel pairs can be chosen. From each set of four parallel diagonals, six different parallel pairs can be chosen. Therefore, the total number of pairs of parallel diagonals is $5 \times 3 + 5 \times 6 = 45$.

Problem 4

In a regular pentagon, we can inscribe a triangle such that one side is a side of the pentagon and the other two sides are diagonals of the pentagon. How many such triangles can be drawn this way? How many can be drawn in a regular *n*-gon, where *n* can be any number?

Any side of the pentagon can form the base of a triangle. For each side, there are two diagonals that can form the other sides of the triangle. Therefore, one triangle can be formed per side, for a total of five triangles.

- 40 -

For each side in a hexagon, there are two possible pairs of diagonals that can form the other sides of the triangle. For example, to make a triangle whose base is side AB in hexagon $ABCDEF$, the other two sides can be made by connecting points A and B to point D or to point E. (Points B and F are off limits because those vertices are each connected to B or A along a side of the hexagon, rather than a diagonal.) So two triangles per side can be made, for a total of twelve.

In general, we can see that for each side of a polygon, the vertices "next to" that side can't be used as the third vertex of the triangle, but any other vertex can. So for each of the n sides, there are $n - 4$ possible triangles, for a total of $n(n - 4) = n^2 - 4n$ triangles.

Problem 5

A ramp with a 30° angle from the ground is to be built up to a 2-foot-high platform. What will be the length of the ramp? How far from the platform will it extend, to the nearest inch?

The ramp, the ground, and the vertical side of the platform make a 30-60 right triangle; the ramp forms the hypotenuse of the triangle, and the side of the platform is the short leg because it is opposite the 30° angle. Therefore, the length of the ramp is twice the height of the platform, or 4 feet. The distance the ramp extends along the ground is the long leg of the triangle, so it is $2\sqrt{3}$ feet. Multiplying $2\sqrt{3}$ feet by 12 gives us $24\sqrt{3}$ inches, which is approximately 42 inches.

Support for circumference of a circle formula

Use transformations to show the ratio between the diameter of a circle and the distance around the circle is a constant, π: $\frac{C_\odot}{d} = \pi$. As the circle is rotated and translated, the circle moves along the line that is just over three times the length of the diameter. $C_\odot = \pi d = 2\pi r$.

Support for area of a circle formula

Use dissection to show that narrow sectors of the circle can be arranged to fit inside a parallelogram with height r and base πr. Using an informal limit, as the number of sectors increases and approaches a very large number, the dissection becomes more accurate and the difference between the area of the parallelogram and the area of the circle will get smaller. $A_\odot = \pi r^2$.

Support for volume of a cylinder formula

Using Cavalieri's principle, consider a cylinder and all the planes which intersect that cylinder parallel to the base. In each plane, there is a circle congruent to all the other circles in all the other planes. Since the circles are all congruent, they all have the same dimensions and the same areas. When all those circles are stacked together, the resulting solid, the cylinder, has a volume equal to the height of the stack times the area of the base. $V_{cylinder} = B \cdot h = \pi r^2 h$.

Support for volume of a pyramid formula

Consider a pyramid and a prism with the same altitude and the same base. The area of the prism is $A_{prism} = B \cdot h$ where B is the area of the base and h is the length of the altitude. Notice in the figures, that the pyramid appears to be inside the prism; this indicates that the volume of the pyramid will be less than the volume of the prism. Also notice that there are three different pyramids inside the prism. The first pyramid uses the front vertical edge as its altitude. The second pyramid uses the left vertical edge as its altitude. The third pyramid is the most difficult to see because it is between the other two. The third pyramid uses the right vertical edge as its altitude.

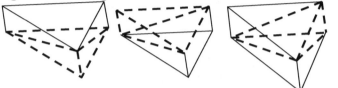

Since there are three pyramids inside the prism, all with the same base and the same altitude, the volume of each pyramid is $\frac{1}{3}$ the volume of the entire prism.

$V_{pyramid} = \frac{1}{3} B \cdot h.$

Support for volume of a cone formula

A pyramid and a cone are similar solids because the cross sections of both become smaller and smaller as they are taken farther and farther from the base.

The volume of a pyramid is $\frac{1}{3} B \cdot h$ where B is the area of the base. If the base of a pyramid is a polygon with n sides, then, using an informal limit, as n increases and approaches a very large number, the shape of the base begins to be like a circle. As shown in the figure to the right, even the change from 6 sides to 8 sides makes a much closer approximation of a circle. So the volume of a cone is also $\frac{1}{3} B \cdot h$ where $B = \pi r^2$.

$V_{cone} = \frac{1}{3} B \cdot h = \frac{1}{3} \pi r^2 h.$

Support for volume of a sphere formula

Consider a cross section of the sphere, not at the center: a circle with radius, c. This circle is a specific distance a from the center of the sphere. These two distances form a right triangle with the radius of the sphere which goes from the center of the sphere to the edge of the circle, so $a^2 + c^2 = r^2$ or $c^2 = r^2 - a^2$. The area of the cross section can be written as a function of the height and radius within the sphere. $A_{cross\ section} = \pi c^2 = \pi(r^2 - a^2) = \pi r^2 - \pi a^2$.

Consider also a cross section of cylinder with from which two congruent cones with tips touching in the cylinder's center have been removed. Again, let a represent the distance of the cross section's center from the center of the cylinder. The cross section through the cylinder is a circle with radius r from which a circle of radius a has been removed:

$A_{cross\ section} = \pi r^2 - \pi a^2$.

Notice that the areas of the cross sections are the same. By Cavalieri's principle, the volumes of the sphere and of the cylinder with cones removed are therefore also the same. The volume of the cylinder without the cones removed is $V = Bh = \pi r^2(2r) = 2\pi r^3$. The

- 42 -

volume of each cone is $V = \frac{1}{3}Bh = \frac{1}{3}\pi r^2(r) = \frac{1}{3}\pi r^3$. So, the volume of the cylinder with both cones removed, and therefore the volume of the sphere with radius r, is $2\pi r^3 - 2\left(\frac{1}{3}\pi r^3\right) = \frac{6}{3}\pi r^3 - \frac{2}{3}\pi r^3 = \frac{4}{3}\pi r^3$.

A sphere example:

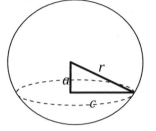

Cavalieri's principle

Cavalieri's principle states that the volumes of two solids are the same if the areas of their corresponding cross sections are equal.

Euclidean, elliptic, and hyperbolic geometry

Euclidean geometry depends on Euclid's postulates, particularly the fourth or "parallel" postulate, which states that given a line and a point not on the line, there is exactly one line parallel to the given line that passes through the given point.

Elliptic and hyperbolic geometry both have different postulates in place of this one. In elliptic geometry, "points" and "lines" are defined in such a way that there are no parallel lines at all. This model describes the geometry of the surface of a sphere: if a "line" is a great circle wrapping around the circumference of the sphere, then any two lines must intersect each other.

In hyperbolic geometry, by contrast, "points" and "lines" are defined so that given a point and a line, there are infinitely many parallel lines passing through the point. The interior of a circle can be described with hyperbolic geometry if a "line" is defined as an arc whose ends both rest on the circle.

Conjecture and theorem

A conjecture is a hypothesis or educated guess about a general rule of mathematics; it is a generalization based on observation of multiple specific cases. For example, if we see many isosceles triangles whose base angles are congruent, we might conjecture that the base angles of every isosceles triangle are congruent. A conjecture, however, is not known for certain to be true.

A theorem is a conjecture that has been proven using mathematical reasoning, based on other theorems that have already been proven, which are ultimately based on the fundamental axioms of whichever mathematical system we are using. For example, we can prove that the base angles of an isosceles triangle must always be congruent, based on applying the rules of mathematical logic to the other properties of triangles we already know.

Converse, inverse, and contrapositive

Example problems
Problem 1: Given statement T: "All four-sided plane figures are rectangles," list the converse, inverse, and contrapositive of statement T. For each of the four statements, state whether it is true or false.

> The converse of statement T is "All rectangles are four-sided plane figures." This is true by definition; a rectangle is defined as a four-sided figure with four right angles.

> The inverse of statement T is "All non-four-sided plane figures are not rectangles." This is also true; a figure that does not have four sides cannot be a rectangle.

> The contrapositive of statement T is "All non-rectangles are not four-sided plane figures." This is false; a rhombus can be a non-rectangle, but it is still a four-sided figure.

> Statement T itself, "All four-sided plane figures are rectangles," is also false. Again, consider a rhombus, which is four-sided but is usually not also a rectangle.

Problem 2: Can a statement and its converse both be true? Can a statement be true and its contrapositive be false?

> A statement and its converse are not necessarily both true or both false, but they can be. For example, the statements "All three-sided plane figures are triangles" and "All triangles are three-sided plane figures" are converses, and they are both true by definition.
> However, a statement and its contrapositive are logically equivalent; a statement cannot be true if its contrapositive is false, or vice versa. Consider the statement "If you are under 18, you are not eligible to vote." If it is true, then the contrapositive, "If you are eligible to vote, you are 18 or over," must also be true; for it to be false, there would have to be people who are eligible to vote who are not yet 18, and that would make the original statement also false.

Proving a conjecture true or false

When a conjecture is universal—that is, of the form "X is always true in situation Y"—then a single example cannot prove it true. You would have to look at every possible example of situation Y and show that X is true in all those examples, or show that there is a logical reason why X *must* always be true in that situation. However, a single counterexample can prove the conjecture false; you only need to show one example of X not being true in situation Y to invalidate the conjecture. On the other hand, when a conjecture is of the form "X is *possible* in situation Y," the opposite holds true. This is because the conjecture is

- 44 -

basically the opposite of "X is always false in situation Y." To prove that X is always false in situation Y would take logical reasoning or an exhaustive list of examples, while it would take only one example to prove that X is *not* always false and hence is possible.

Proving that angles add up to 180°

Example problems
Problem 1: Prove that the angles of a triangle add up to 180°.

> Consider triangle *ABC*; now imagine line *DAE*, which goes through *A* and is parallel to *BC*. Angles *DAB* and *ABC* are alternate interior angles, so they are congruent; the same is true for angles *EAC* and *ACB*. And since angles *DAB*, *BAC*, and *EAC* all lie on a line together, their total measure is 180°. Therefore, substituting *ABC* for the congruent angle *DAB* and *ACB* for the congruent angle *EAC*, we can see that angles *ABC*, *BAC*, and *ACB*, the three interior angles of the triangle, add up to 180°.

Problem 2: Prove that the angles of an *n*-gon, where *n* can be any whole number greater than 2, add up to (n-2)180°.

> First, consider a quadrilateral, and notice that it can be divided into two triangles by drawing one diagonal across it. The interior angles of the two triangles each add up to 180°, and the interior angles of the quadrilateral are made up by adding up the angles of the triangles; hence the interior angles of the quadrilateral measure a total of 360°.
>
> Next, consider doing the same thing with a pentagon. Drawing two diagonals from the same vertex divides the pentagon into three triangles. Since each triangle's angles measure 180°, the pentagon's angles must sum to three times that amount, or 540°.
> In general, you can see that any *n*-gon can be divided up into *n* – 2 triangles by drawing *n* – 3 diagonals from one vertex. Therefore, any *n*-gon's angles sum to (*n*-2) times 180°.

Diagonals

Example problems
Problem 1: Which of these statements are true?
The diagonals of a parallelogram (1) are congruent, (2) are perpendicular, (3) bisect each other.
The diagonals of a rectangle (1) are congruent, (2) are perpendicular, (3) bisect each other.
The diagonals of a rhombus (1) are congruent, (2) are perpendicular, (3) bisect each other.

> The diagonals of a parallelogram aren't necessarily congruent (because some rhombuses' aren't) or perpendicular (because some rectangles' aren't), but they do bisect each other. This is because they divide the parallelogram into four triangles which can be shown to be congruent by AAA.

The diagonals of a rectangle aren't perpendicular unless the rectangle is a square. They are congruent, however. Consider right triangles ABC and BAD, each of which is half of rectangle ABCD. Legs AB and BA are congruent, and so are legs BC and AD; therefore, hypotenuses AC and BD, the diagonals of the rectangle, are congruent. The diagonals of a rectangle also bisect each other, because all rectangles are also parallelograms.

The diagonals of a rhombus aren't necessarily congruent (consider a long, skinny rhombus), but they are perpendicular and bisect each other. Consider rhombus ABCD. Because B and D are both equidistant from A and C, the line through B and D must be the perpendicular bisector of segment AC. Similarly, because A and C are both equidistant from B and D, the line through A and C must be the perpendicular bisector of segment BD.

Problem 2: The diagonals of a quadrilateral (1) are congruent, (2) are perpendicular, (3) bisect each other.
The diagonals of a trapezoid (1) are congruent, (2) are perpendicular, (3) bisect each other.
The diagonals of a kite (1) are congruent, (2) are perpendicular, (3) bisect each other.

Quadrilaterals come in many different shapes, and no generalizations can be made about whether their diagonals are congruent, are perpendicular, or bisect each other.

Trapezoids have one pair of parallel sides, but this does not mean their diagonals are necessarily congruent, perpendicular, or bisect each other.

Kites have two pairs of adjacent sides that are congruent, and this means that their diagonals must be perpendicular. Consider kite ABCD with AB and BC as one pair of congruent sides, and CD and DA as the other. Because B and D are both equidistant from A and C, the line through B and D must be the perpendicular bisector of segment AC. So the diagonals of a kite are perpendicular, and one bisects the other, but they don't necessarily both bisect each other, and they may not be congruent.

Angle bisectors

<u>Example problem</u>
Prove that the angle bisectors of a triangle all meet at one point.

Consider triangle ABC, with ray AD bisecting angle A, ray BE bisecting angle B, and ray CF bisecting angle C. An important property of angle bisectors is that every point on the ray bisecting an angle is equidistant from the rays that make up the angle; for example, for any point on AD, the shortest distance from that point to AB is equal to the shortest distance from that same point to AC.
So, consider point P, where AD and BE meet. Because P is on AD, the shortest distance from P to AB equals the shortest distance from P to AC; similarly, because P is on BE, the shortest distance from P to AB equals the shortest distance from P to BC. Therefore, by the transitive property, the shortest distance from P to AC equals the shortest distance from P to BC—and that

means that *P* also lies on *CF*. So, the third angle bisector meets the other two at the same point where they meet each other.

Complementary, supplementary, and adjacent angles

Complementary: Two angles whose sum is exactly 90°. The two angles may or may not be adjacent. In a right triangle, the two acute angles are complementary.

Supplementary: Two angles whose sum is exactly 180°. The two angles may or may not be adjacent. Two intersecting lines always form two pairs of supplementary angles. Adjacent supplementary angles will always form a straight line.

Adjacent: Two angles that have the same vertex and share a side. Vertical angles are not adjacent because they share a vertex but no common side.

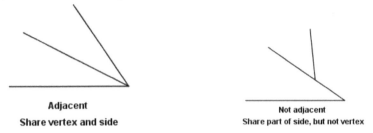

Adjacent
Share vertex and side

Not adjacent
Share part of side, but not vertex

Intersecting lines, parallel lines, vertical angles, and transversals

Intersecting Lines: Lines that have exactly one point in common.

Parallel Lines: Lines in the same plane that have no points in common and never meet. It is possible for lines to be in different planes, have no points in common, and never meet, but they are not parallel because they are in different planes.

Vertical Angles: Non-adjacent angles formed when two lines intersect. Vertical angles are congruent. In the diagram, $\angle ABD \cong \angle CBE$ and $\angle ABC \cong \angle DBE$.

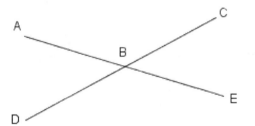

Transversal: A straight line that intersects at least two other lines, which may or may not be parallel.

Congruent and similar figures

Congruent figures are geometric figures that have the same size and shape. All corresponding angles are equal, and all corresponding sides are equal. It is indicated by the symbol ≅.

Similar figures are geometric figures that have the same shape, but do not necessarily have the same size. All corresponding angles are equal, and all corresponding sides are proportional, but they do not have to be equal. It is indicated by the symbol ~.

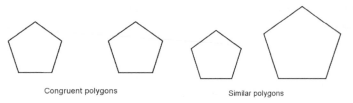

Congruent polygons   Similar polygons

Note that all congruent figures are also similar, but not all similar figures are congruent.

Symmetry, symmetric, and line of symmetry

Line of Symmetry: The line that divides a figure or object into two symmetric parts. Each symmetric half is congruent to the other. An object may have no lines of symmetry, one line of symmetry, or more than one line of symmetry.

No lines of symmetry   One line of symmetry   More than one line of symmetry

Ray, angle, and vertex

A ray is a portion of a line extending from a point in one direction. It has a definite beginning, but no ending.

An angle is formed when two rays meet at a common point. It may be a common starting point, or it may be the intersection of rays, lines, and/or line segments.

A vertex is the point at which two segments or rays meet to form an angle. If the angle is formed by intersecting rays, lines, and/or line segments, the vertex is the point at which four angles are formed.

Perpendicular lines and perpendicular bisectors

Perpendicular lines are lines that intersect at right angles. They are represented by the symbol ⊥. The shortest distance from a line to a point not on the line is a perpendicular segment from the point to the line.

In a plane, the perpendicular bisector of a line segment is a line comprised of the set of all points that are equidistant from the endpoints of the segment. This line always forms a right angle with the segment in the exact middle of the segment. Note that you can only find perpendicular bisectors of segments.

Preimage, image, translation, reflection, rotation, and dilation

Preimage: The original unchanged image in its original position.

Image: A unique set of points

Translation: A case where a geometric image is slid, usually horizontally or vertically. The resulting image is congruent to the original image, but has been moved in a straight line.

Reflection: A case where a geometric image is flipped across a line of reflection. The resulting image is congruent to and a mirror image of the original image.

Rotation: A case where a geometric image is rotated around the center of rotation to a new position. The new image is congruent to the original image, but has been turned to a new position.

Dilation: A case where a geometric image has been expanded or contracted by a scale factor. The resulting image is similar to the original image, but not congruent.

Projection of a point on a line and projection of a segment on a line

The projection of a point on a line is the point at which a perpendicular line drawn from the given point to the given line intersects the line. This is also the shortest distance from the given point to the line.

The projection of a segment on a line is a segment whose endpoints are the points formed when perpendicular lines are drawn from the endpoints of the given segment to the given line. This is similar to the length a diagonal line *appears* to be when viewed from above.

Point

A *point* is a specific location and is used to help understand and define all other concepts in geometry. A point is denoted by a single capital letter, such as point P.

 P

Angle

Angle – The set of points which are part of two lines that intersect at a specific point. An angle is made up of two "half lines" called rays that begin at the shared point, called the vertex, and extend away from that point. An angle can be denoted simply by the angle's vertex ($\angle A$ or $\angle A$) or by three points: one from one ray, the point of intersection, and one from the second ray ($\angle BAC$ or $\angle BAC$).

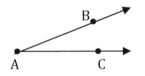

Circle

Circle – A continuous set of points which are all equidistant from a separate point called the center. A circle usually shares the same label as its center: circle P with center at point P.

Perpendicular lines

Perpendicular lines – Two lines which intersect at one specific point and create four 90° angles. Notation: $\overleftrightarrow{DE} \perp \overleftrightarrow{EF}$ when lines DE and EF intersect and form right angles at point E.

Parallel lines

Parallel lines – Two lines which do not share any points and never intersect. Notation: $\overleftrightarrow{GH} \parallel \overleftrightarrow{IJ}$.

Line segment

Line segment – The section of a line that is between two specific points on that line, usually denoted by two points: $\overline{KL}$.

Respresenting transformations

Transparencies

After drawing a shape on a piece of transparency, the shape can be rotated by leaving the transparency on a flat surface and turning it clockwise or counterclockwise.

After drawing a shape on a piece of transparency, the shape can be translated by leaving the transparency on a flat surface and sliding it in any direction (left, right, up, down, or along a diagonal).

After drawing a shape on a piece of transparency, the shape can be reflected by turning the transparency over so that the side the shape is on the underside of the transparency, touching the table.

Functions to represent a translation on the Cartesian plane

First, determine the points which define the shape. Second, use an equation or equations to express how the vertices of the shape are moving. When the shape is translated both vertically and horizontally, the translation can be expressed using two equations: one for the x-values and one for the y-values.

For example, consider a triangle, which is defined by its vertices at three specific ordered pairs. Adding 5 to each of the x-values will create a second triangle five units to the right of the first triangle; the equation representing this transformation is $x_2 = x_1 + 5$, where x_1 represents the x-coordinates of the original triangle and x_2 represents the x-coordinates of the translated triangle. If the triangle is also moved four units downward, the equation $y_2 = y_1 - 4$ can be used to find the new y=coordinates, represented by y_2, from the triangle's original y-coordinates, represented by y_1. Together, the horizontal and vertical shift can be written as $\begin{cases} x_2 = x_1 + 5 \\ y_2 = y_1 - 4 \end{cases}$, and these equations would be used to transform each vertex like so:

first point (x_1, y_1)	first vertex (3,6)
x-values: $x_2 = x_1 + 5$	$x_2 = 3 + 5 = 8$
y-values: $y_2 = y_1 - 4$	$y_2 = 6 - 4 = 2$
new point (x_2, y_2)	first vertex (8,2)
second vertex (5,1)	third vertex (4, −1)
$x_2 = 5 + 5 = 10$	$x_2 = 4 + 5 = 9$
$y_2 = 1 - 4 = -3$	$y_2 = -1 - 4 = -5$
second vertex (10, −3)	third vertex (9, −5)

Size and shape when translated or stretched horizontally

When a figure is translated, it moves to another location within the plane; since each point is shifted by the same distance, its size and shape remain the same. When a figure is stretched horizontally, its size and shape are affected. For example, consider an equilateral triangle which has a horizontal base. If the two endpoints of the base are pulled horizontally in opposite directions, the angle opposite the base widens as the two other angles become smaller. So, the lengths of the sides and the angle measures change, and the resulting triangle differs in both size and shape from the original triangle.

Transformations that carry a figure onto itself

Rectangle
A rectangle will be carried onto itself when it is rotated any multiple of 180° either clockwise or counterclockwise about its center. If the rectangle is a square, a rotation of 90° or any multiple of 90° clockwise or counterclockwise about the center will carry the square onto itself.
Any rectangle will be carried onto itself when it is rotated 360° or any multiple of 360° about any point either clockwise or counterclockwise.
A rectangle will also be carried onto itself when it is reflected over any of its lines of symmetry. A rectangle has two lines of symmetry, and a square has four.

Parallelogram
A parallelogram will be carried onto itself when it is rotated by any multiple of 180° either clockwise or counterclockwise about its center. A square or any other rhombus is carried onto itself when it is rotated about its center by a multiple of 90°. Any parallelogram will be carried onto itself when it is rotated 360° or any multiple of 360° about any point either clockwise or counterclockwise.

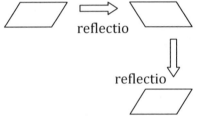

reflectio

reflectio

A square or other rhombus reflected across any of its four lines of symmetry will map onto itself, and a rectangle reflected across either of its two line of symmetry will be carried onto itself. Other parallelograms have no lines of symmetry and can therefore not be reflected onto themselves

Trapezoid
A trapezoid will be carried onto itself when it is rotated 360° or any multiple of 360° either clockwise or counterclockwise.

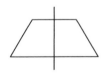

A trapezoid will be carried onto itself when it is reflected over its line of symmetry, which is the perpendicular bisector of its two parallel sides.

Regular polygon
A regular polygon will be carried onto itself when it is rotated about its center either clockwise or counterclockwise by $360°/n$, where n is the number of sides of the polygon.

Any polygon will be carried onto itself when it is rotated 360° or any multiple of 360° about any point either clockwise or counterclockwise.

A regular polygon will be carried onto itself when it is reflected over any of its lines of symmetry.

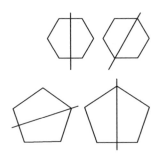

Rotation, center of rotation, and angle of rotation

A rotation is a transformation that turns a figure around a point called the center of rotation, which can lie anywhere in the plane. If a line is drawn from a point on a figure to the center of rotation, and another line is drawn from the center to the rotated image of that point, the angle between the two lines is the angle of rotation. The vertex of the angle of rotation is the center of rotation.

Reflection over a line and reflection in a point

A reflection of a figure over a line (a "flip") creates a congruent image that is the same distance from the line as the original figure but on the opposite side. The line of reflection is the perpendicular bisector of any line segment drawn from a point on the original figure to its reflected image (unless the point and its reflected image happen to be the same point, which happens when a figure is reflected over one of its own sides).
A reflection of a figure in a point is the same as the rotation of the figure 180° about that point. The image of the figure is congruent to the original figure. The point of reflection is the midpoint of a line segment which connects a point in the figure to its image (unless the point and its reflected image happen to be the same point, which happens when a figure is reflected in one of its own points).

Translation

A translation is a transformation which slides a figure from one position in the plane to another position in the plane. The original figure and the translated figure have the same size, shape, and orientation.

Rotation, reflection, and translation

To rotate a given figure: 1. Identify the point of rotation. 2. Using tracing paper, geometry software, or by approximation, recreate the figure at a new location around the point of rotation.

To reflect a given figure: 1. Identify the line of reflection. 2. By folding the paper, using geometry software, or by approximation, recreate the image at a new location on the other side of the line of reflection.

To translate a given figure: 1. Identify the new location. 2. Using graph paper, geometry software, or by approximation, recreate the figure in the new location. If using graph paper, make a chart of the x- and y-values to keep track of the coordinates of all critical points.

Dilation

Dilation is a transformation which proportionally stretches or shrinks a figure by a scale factor. The dilated image is the same shape and orientation as the original image but a different size. A polygon and its dilated image are similar.

Identifying transformation

To identify that a figure has been rotated, look for evidence that the figure is still face-up, but has changed its orientation.

To identify that a figure has been reflected across a line, look for evidence that the figure is now face-down.

To identify that a figure has been translated, look for evidence that a figure is still face-up and has not changed orientation; the only change is location.

To identify that a figure has been dilated, look for evidence that the figure has changed its size but not its orientation.

Line

A line is a straight continuous set of points and usually denoted by two points in that set. For instance, $\overleftrightarrow{AB}$ is the line which passes through points A and B.

Distance along a line and distance around a circular arc

The distance along a line, or the distance between two points on a line, can be measured using a ruler. If the two points are located on the Cartesian plane, the distance can be found using the distance formula: $d = \sqrt{(x_2 - x_1)^2 + (y_2 - y_1)^2}$.

The distance around a circular arc, or the distance along a circle between two points, can be measured using a piece of string (to follow the shape of the circle) and then a ruler. The distance can also be found by finding the portion of the circle's circumference represented by the arc.

Comparing similar figures

Example problems

Problem1: Triangle *ABC* is similar to triangle *EDF*. If *AB* is 9 inches, *BC* is 8 inches, *EF* is 9 inches, and *DF* is 12 inches, what are the measures of *AC* and *DE*?

> If *ABC* is similar to *EDF*, that means the ratios of the corresponding side lengths are equal, the corresponding sides being *AB* and *ED*, *BC* and *DF*, and *AC* and *EF* respectively. The only pair of which we know both side lengths is *BC* and *DF*; the ratio of those two sides is 8:12, or 2:3. Therefore, the ratio of

AB to *ED* is 2:3, or 9:13.5, so the length of *ED* (which is also *DE*) is 13.5 inches. The ratio of *AC* to *EF* is also 2:3, or 6:9, so side AC measures 6 inches.

Problem 2: The plane figures *ABCDE* and *FGHJK* are similar. If the angles *ABC, GHJ, BCD, HJK,* and *DEA* measure 120°, 100°, 100°, 120°, and 140°, respectively, what are the measures of the remaining angles?

Since the figures are similar, their corresponding angles must be congruent. Specifically, angles *ABC* and *FGH* are congruent, as are angles *BCD* and *GHJ, CDE* and *HJK, DEA* and *JKF,* and *EAB* and *KFG.* Therefore, angles *ABC* and *FGH* both measure 120°, *BCD* and *GHJ* both measure 100°, *CDE* and *HJK* both measure 120°, *DEA* and *JKF* both measure 140°, and the only angle measures still missing are those of angles *EAB* and *KFG.*

Because ABCDE and FGHJK are pentagons, their internal angle measures must sum to 540°. The known angles of each pentagon so far sum to 120 + 100 + 120 + 140 = 480°, so the remaining angle of each pentagon must measure 60°.

Problem 3: Triangles *ABC* and *HJK* are similar. If the coordinates of points *A, B,* and *C* are (2, 5), (1, -2), and (-3, 6), respectively, and the coordinates of points *H* and *J* are (3, 2.5) and (0.5, -15), respectively, what are the coordinates of point *K*?

The horizontal distance between *H* and *J* is 2.5 times the horizontal distance between *A* and *B*; similarly, the vertical distance between *H* and *J* is 2.5 times the vertical distance between *A* and *B*. We don't need to find the actual lengths of the sides of both triangles; we just need to know that the sides of *HJK* will be 2.5 times as long in both the horizontal and vertical directions as the corresponding sides of *ABC.* Since *C* is 4 units left and 8 units up from *B*, *K* must therefore be 10 units left and 20 units up from *J.* The coordinates of *K,* then, are (-9.5, 5). We can check this answer by comparing the distance between *H* and *K* with the distance between *A* and *C*; it should also be 2.5 times as far in both directions.

Changing the width and length of a rectangle

<u>Example problem</u>
If the length and width of a rectangle are both doubled, what happens to the rectangle's area? Its perimeter?
If the length is doubled while the width is tripled, what happens to the area and to the perimeter?

Algebraic reasoning is the best way to approach this problem. If the original length and width of the rectangle are represented as *l* and *w*, then the original area is *lw* and the perimeter is 2(*l* + *w*). After doubling, the new length and width are 2*l* and 2*w*, so the new area is 2*l* × 2*w* or 4*lw*, and the new perimeter is 2(2*l* + 2*w*), or 4(*l* + *w*). The new area is four times the old area, and the new perimeter is two times the old perimeter.

On the other hand, if the length is doubled (becoming 2*l*) while the width is tripled (becoming 3*w*), the new area is 2*l* × 3*w* or 6*lw*, and the new perimeter is 2(2*l* + 3*w*), which cannot be simplified further. The new area is six times the old area, but the new perimeter does not have any particular relationship to the old perimeter.

Parallel lines with a transversal

<u>Interior angles, exterior angles, and corresponding angles</u>
Interior Angles: When two parallel lines are cut by a transversal, the angles that are between the two parallel lines are interior angles. In the diagram below, angles 3, 4, 5, and 6 are interior angles.
Exterior Angles: When two parallel lines are cut by a transversal, the angles that are outside the parallel lines are exterior angles. In the diagram below, angles 1, 2, 7, and 8 are exterior angles.
Corresponding Angles: When two parallel lines are cut by a transversal, the angles that are in the same position relative to the transversal and one of the parallel lines. The diagram below has four pairs of corresponding angles: angles 1 and 5; angles 2 and 6; angles 3 and 7; and angles 4 and 8. Corresponding angles formed by parallel lines are congruent.

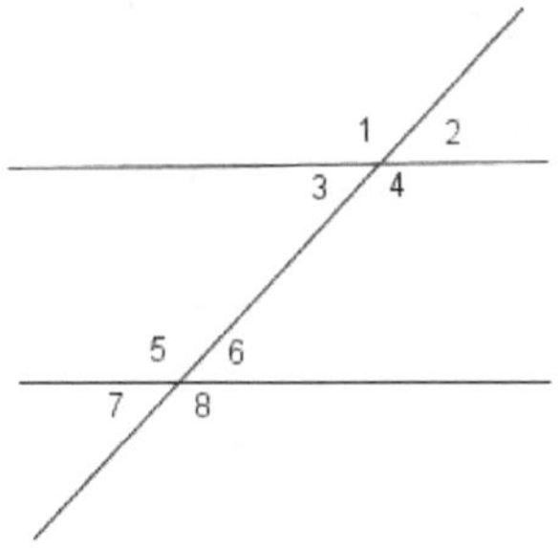

<u>Alternate interior angles and alternate exterior angles</u>
Alternate Interior Angles: When two parallel lines are cut by a transversal, two interior angles that are on opposite sides of the transversal and on opposite parallel lines are congruent opposite interior angles. In the diagram below, there are two pair of alternate interior angles: angles 3 and 6, and angles 4 and 5. Alternate interior angles formed by parallel lines are congruent.
Alternate Exterior Angles: When two parallel lines are cut by a transversal, two exterior angles that are on opposite sides of the transversal and on opposite parallel lines are congruent opposite exterior angles. In the diagram below, there are two pair of alternate exterior angles: angles 1 and 8, and angles 2 and 7. Alternate exterior angles formed by parallel lines are congruent.

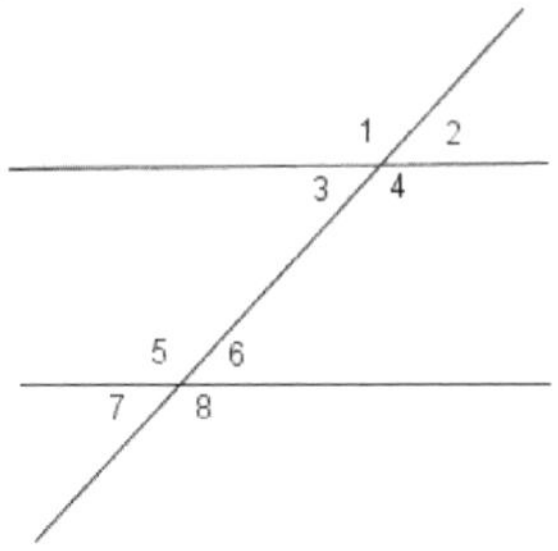

Types of angles

The six types of angles based on angle measurement are as follows:
- An acute is an angle with a degree measure less than 90°.
- A right angle is an angle with a degree measure of exactly 90°.
- An obtuse angle is an angle with a degree measure greater than 90° but less than 180°.
- A straight angle is an angle with a degree measure of exactly 180°. This is also a semicircle.
- A reflex angle is an angle with a degree measure greater than 180° but less than 360°.
- A full angle is an angle with a degree measure of exactly 360°. This is also a circle.

Plane

A plane is a two-dimensional flat surface defined by three non-collinear points. A plane extends an infinite distance in all directions in those two dimensions. It contains an infinite number of points, parallel lines and segments, intersecting lines and segments, as well as parallel or intersecting rays. A plane will never contain a three-dimensional figure or skew lines. A plane may intersect a circular conic surface, such as a cone, to form conic sections, such as the parabola, hyperbola, circle or ellipse. Two given planes will either be parallel or they will intersect to form a line.

Proving circles are similar

Similar figures have the same shape but not necessarily the same size. Similar polygons have congruent corresponding angles and proportional sides. To extend this idea to circles, consider an arbitrary number of points along the circle. If points are chosen in such a way that the angles created by the radii to those points are congruent when measured from a horizontal radius, then the corresponding angles are congruent. If the ratios of corresponding radii are found and compared, the results would be proportional, thus all circles are similar.

Central angles and inscribed angles and central angles and circumscribed angles

All of these angles have rays which pass through the same points on the circle at B and C. A central angle's vertex is at the same point as the center of a circle. An inscribed angle's vertex is on a point on the circle. A circumscribed angle's vertex is outside the circle, and its rays are tangent to the circle.

$m\angle BDC = \frac{1}{2} \cdot m\angle BAC$
$m\angle BEC = 180 - m\angle BAC$

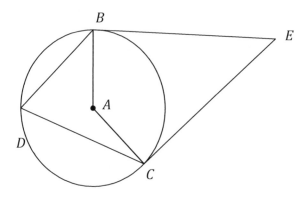

Inscribed angles whose endpoints lie on a diameter

The measure of all inscribed angles is equal to half the intercepted arc. Since a diameter creates an arc of 180°, all inscribed angles whose endpoints lie on a diameter have a measure of 90°, are right angles, and are congruent.

Tangent and the radius at the point of tangency

A tangent intersects a circle at only one point. The radius is a line segment from the center of the circle to a point on a circle. A tangent is perpendicular to the radius at the point of tangency.

Construction of a circle inscribed in a triangle

Given a triangle, construct the angle bisectors of each of its angles. Place the compass tip on one of the vertices, open the compass and draw an arc that intersects both rays of the angle. Open the compass a little further and move the stationary end to one of the side-arc intersections. Make a small arc beyond the first arc. Without changing the compass opening, move the stationary end to the other side-arc intersection. Make another small arc that intersects the last small arc. Use a straightedge to draw a line through the angle vertex and the point of intersection for the two small arcs. Repeat these steps for the other two vertices of the triangle. The point where the three angle bisectors intersect is called the incenter. The incenter is equidistant from all three sides of the triangle.

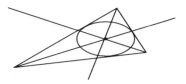

Construction of a circle circumscribed around a triangle

Construct the perpendicular bisector of each side of the triangle. Place the compass tip on one of the vertices, open the compass past the middle of the side, and draw an arc that extends both inside and outside the triangle. Without changing the compass opening, move to the other endpoint of the side and draw another arc that intersects the first. Use the straightedge to draw the line that connects the two intersections of the arcs and that is perpendicular to the side it bisects. Repeat these steps for the other two sides of the triangle.

The point where the perpendicular bisectors intersect is called the circumcenter. The circumcenter is equidistant from all three vertices of the triangle. Place the compass tip on the circumcenter and open the compass so the pencil is touching one of the vertices. Draw a circle around the triangle, noting that the circle touches the triangle at each of its vertices.

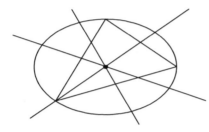

Sum of the measures of opposite angles in a quadrilateral inscribed in a circle

Since quadrilateral $ABCD$ is inscribed in circle P, angles A, B, C, and D are all inscribed in circle P.

The measure of an inscribed angle is equal to half the arc it intercepts. Angle A intercepts $\widehat{BCD}$ and angle C intercepts $\widehat{DAB}$.	$m\angle A = \dfrac{1}{2} \cdot m\widehat{BCD} \;\rightarrow\; m\widehat{BCD} = 2 \cdot m\angle A$ $m\angle C = \dfrac{1}{2} \cdot m\widehat{DAB} \;\rightarrow\; m\widehat{DAB} = 2 \cdot m\angle C$
$\widehat{BCD}$ and $\widehat{DAB}$ are two arcs that form a whole circle.	$m\widehat{BCD} + m\widehat{DAB} = 360°$
Use substitution.	$2 \cdot m\angle A + 2 \cdot m\angle C = 360°$
Use the distributive property and divide by 2.	$2 \cdot (m\angle A + m\angle C) = 360°$ $m\angle A + m\angle C = 180°$

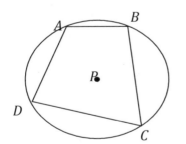

Construction of a tangent line from a point outside a circle to the circle

Consider $\odot C$ and a point A outside of circle C. First, use a straightedge to construct $\overline{AC}$. Find M, the midpoint of $\overline{AC}$. Place the compass tip on point M and draw a circle through C. These two points of intersection (points B and D) are both points of tangency. Use a straightedge to construct a line through either point of tangency and point A. This line is tangent to circle C from a point outside the circle.

Center, radius, and diameter

Center: A single point that is equidistant from every point on a circle. (Point O in the diagram below.)
Radius: A line segment that joins the center of the circle and any one point on the circle. All radii of a circle are equal. (Segments OX, OY, and OZ in the diagram below.)
Diameter: A line segment that passes through the center of the circle and has both endpoints on the circle. The length of the diameter is exactly twice the length of the radius. (Segment XZ in the diagram below.)

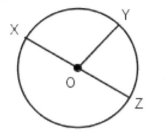

Inscribed and circumscribed

A circle is inscribed in a polygon if each of the sides of the polygon is tangent to the circle. A polygon is inscribed in a circle if each of the vertices of the polygon lies on the circle.
A circle is circumscribed about a polygon if each of the vertices of the polygon lies on the circle. A polygon is circumscribed about the circle if each of the sides of the polygon is tangent to the circle.
If one figure is inscribed in another, then the other figure is circumscribed about the first figure.

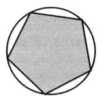

Circle circumscribed about a pentagon
Pentagon inscribed in a circle

Quadrilaterals, parallelograms, and trapezoids

Quadrilateral: A closed two-dimensional geometric figure comprised of exactly four straight sides. The sum of the interior angles of any quadrilateral is 360°.
Parallelogram: A quadrilateral that has exactly two pairs of opposite parallel sides. The sides that are parallel are also congruent. The opposite interior angles are always congruent, and the consecutive interior angles are supplementary. The diagonals of a parallelogram bisect each other. Each diagonal divides the parallelogram into two congruent triangles.

Trapezoid: Traditionally, a quadrilateral that has exactly one pair of parallel sides. Some math texts define trapezoid as a quadrilateral that has at least one pair of parallel sides. Because there are no rules governing the second pair of sides, there are no rules that apply to the properties of the diagonals of a trapezoid.

Rectangles, rhombuses, and squares

Rectangles, rhombuses, and squares are all special forms of parallelograms.
Rectangle: A parallelogram with four right angles. All rectangles are parallelograms, but not all parallelograms are rectangles. The diagonals of a rectangle are congruent.

Rhombus: A parallelogram with four congruent sides. All rhombuses are parallelograms, but not all parallelograms are rhombuses. The diagonals of a rhombus are perpendicular to each other.

Square: A parallelogram with four right angles and four congruent sides. All squares are also parallelograms, rhombuses, and rectangles. The diagonals of a square are congruent and perpendicular to each other.

Side, vertex, regular polygon, apothem, and radius

Each straight line segment of a polygon is called a side.
The point at which two sides of a polygon intersect is called the vertex. In a polygon, the number of sides is always equal to the number of vertices.
A polygon with all sides congruent and all angles equal is called a regular polygon.
A line segment from the center of a polygon perpendicular to a side of the polygon is called the apothem. In a regular polygon, the apothem can be used to find the area of the polygon using the formula $A = \frac{1}{2}ap$, where a is the apothem and p is the perimeter.
A line segment from the center of a polygon to a vertex of the polygon is called the radius. The radius of a regular polygon is also the radius of a circle that can be circumscribed about the polygon.

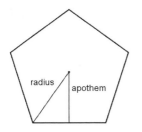

Shapes

The general name for each shape that contains from three sides to ten sides, inclusive, as well as a twelve-sided figure are as follows:

- 3 sides: triangle
- 4 sides: quadrilateral
- 5 sides: pentagon
- 6 sides: hexagon
- 7 sides: heptagon
- 8 sides: octagon
- 9 sides: nonagon
- 10 sides: decagon
- 12 sides: dodecagon
- n sides: n-gon

Diagonal, convex, and concave

A diagonal is a line segment that joins two non-adjacent vertices of a polygon.
A convex polygon is a polygon whose diagonals all lie within the interior of the polygon.
A concave polygon is a polygon with a least one diagonal that lies outside the polygon. In the diagram below, quadrilateral *ABCD* is concave because diagonal $\overline{AC}$ lies outside the polygon.

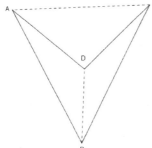

The number of diagonals a polygon has can be found by using the formula: number of diagonals $= \frac{n(n-3)}{2}$, where n is the number of sides in the polygon. This formula works for all polygons, not just regular polygons.

Parallelogram, rhombus, square, and rectangle

A quadrilateral whose diagonals bisect each other is a parallelogram. A quadrilateral whose opposite sides are parallel (2 pairs of parallel sides) is a parallelogram.

A quadrilateral whose diagonals are perpendicular bisectors of each other is a rhombus. A quadrilateral whose opposite sides (both pairs) are parallel and congruent is a rhombus. A parallelogram that has a right angle is a rectangle. (Consecutive angles of a parallelogram are supplementary. Therefore if there is one right angle in a parallelogram, there are four right angles in that parallelogram.)

A rhombus with one right angle is a square. Because the rhombus is a special form of a parallelogram, the rules about the angles of a parallelogram also apply to the rhombus.

Concentric circles, arc, and semicircle

Concentric circles are circles that have the same center, but not the same length of radii. A bulls-eye target is an example of concentric circles. An arc is a portion of a circle. Specifically, an arc is the set of points between and including two points on a circle. An arc does not contain any points inside the circle. When a segment is drawn from the endpoints of an arc to the center of the circle, a sector is formed. A semicircle is an arc whose endpoints are the endpoints of the diameter of a circle. A semicircle is exactly half of a circle.

Chord, secant, tangent, and point of tangency

Chord: A line segment that has both endpoints on a circle. In the diagram below, $\overline{EB}$ is a chord.

Secant: A line that passes through a circle and contains a chord of that circle. In the diagram below, $\overleftrightarrow{EB}$ is a secant and contains chord $\overline{EB}$.

Tangent: A line in the same plane as a circle that touches the circle in exactly one point. While a line segment can be tangent to a circle as part of a line that is tangent, it is improper to say a tangent can be a line segment by itself that touches the circle in exactly one point. In the diagram below, $\overleftrightarrow{CD}$ is tangent to circle A. Notice that $\overline{FB}$ is not tangent to the circle. $\overline{FB}$ is a line segment that touches the circle in exactly one point, but if the segment were extended, it would touch the circle in a second point.

Point of Tangency: The point at which a tangent touches a circle. In the diagram below, point B is the point of tangency.

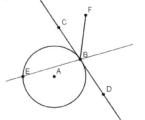

Central angles, major arcs, minor arcs, and semicircle

Central Angle: An angle whose vertex is the center of a circle and whose legs intercept an arc of the circle.

Major Arc: An arc of a circle, having a measure of at least 180°. The measure of the major arc can be found by subtracting the measure of the central angle from 360°.

Minor Arc: An arc of a circle, having a measure less than 180°. The measure of the central angle is equal to the measure of the arc.

Semicircle: An arc having a measure of exactly 180°.

Inscribed angles and intercepted arcs

An inscribed angle is an angle whose vertex lies on a circle and whose legs contain chords of that circle. The portion of the circle intercepted by the legs of the angle is called the intercepted arc. The measure of the intercepted arc is exactly twice the measure of the inscribed angle. In the diagram below, angle ABC is an inscribed angle. arc $AC = 2(m\angle ABC)$

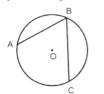

Any angle inscribed in a semicircle is a right angle. The intercepted arc is 180°, making the inscribed angle half that, or 90°. In the diagram below, angle ABC is inscribed in semicircle ABC, making angle B equal to 90°.

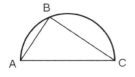

Angles formed by two secants

A secant is a line that intersects a curve in two points. Two secants may intersect inside the circle, on the circle, or outside the circle. When the two secants intersect on the circle, an inscribed angle is formed.

When two secants intersect inside a circle, the measure of each of two vertical angles is equal to half the sum of the two intercepted arcs. In the diagram below, $m\angle AEB = \frac{1}{2}(\text{arc}AB + \text{arc}CD)$ and $m\angle BEC = \frac{1}{2}(\text{arc}BC + \text{arc}AD)$.

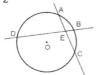

When two secants intersect outside a circle, the measure of the angle formed is equal to half the difference of the two arcs that lie between the two secants. In the diagram below, $m\angle E = \frac{1}{2}(\text{arc}AB - \text{arc}CD)$.

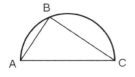

Arc length

The arc length of a circle is the length of a portion of the circumference between two points on the circle. When the arc is defined by two radii forming a central angle, the formula for arc length is $s = r\theta$, where s is the arc length, r is the length of the radius, and θ is the measure of the central angle in radians.

Sector

A sector is the portion of a circle formed by two radii and their intercepted arc. While the arc length is exclusively the points that are also on the circumference of the circle, the sector is the entire area bounded by the arc and the two radii.

Formula for the area of a sector

The area of $\odot\, C$ is πr^2. A circle has $360°$ and a sector is a slice of the circle. The measure of the central angle determines what fraction the sector is of the circle. So, to find the area of the sector, multiply the fraction and the area of the whole circle.

In degrees, $Area_{sector} = \frac{m\angle C}{360} \cdot \pi r^2$.

In radians, $Area_{sector} = \frac{m\angle C}{2\pi} \cdot \pi r^2 = \frac{m\angle C}{2} \cdot r^2$.

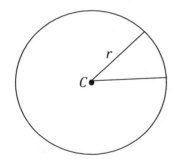

Area and arc length of a sector of a circle

The area of a sector of a circle is found by the formula, $A = \frac{\theta r^2}{2}$, where A is the area, θ is the measure of the central angle in radians, and r is the radius. To find the area when the central angle is in degrees, use the formula, $A = \frac{\theta \pi r^2}{360}$, where θ is the measure of the central angle in degrees and r is the radius.

The arc length of a sector of a circle is found by the formula: arc length $= r\theta$, where r is the radius and θ is the measure of the central angle in radians. To find the arc length when the central angle is given in degrees, use the formula: arc length $= \frac{\theta(2\pi r)}{360}$, where θ is the measure of the central angle in degrees and r is the radius.

- 64 -

Example problems

Problem 1
Use similarity to show the length of an arc intercepted by a central angle is proportional to the radius.

Consider two concentric circles, $\odot C$ with radius r and $\odot C$ with radius R. $\angle ACB$ cuts an arc $(\widehat{AB})$ in the larger circle and a similar arc $(\widehat{DE})$ in the smaller circle. The circumference of a circle is $2\pi r$ and an arc is a piece of the circle. The measure of the central angle determines what fraction the arc is of the circle. So, to find the length of the arc, multiply the fraction and the circumference.

In degrees, $l\widehat{AB} = \frac{m\angle C}{360} \cdot 2\pi R$. In radians, $l\widehat{AB} = \frac{m\angle C}{2\pi} \cdot 2\pi R = m\angle C \cdot R$.

In degrees, $l\widehat{DE} = \frac{m\angle C}{360} \cdot 2\pi r$. In radians, $l\widehat{DE} = \frac{m\angle C}{2\pi} \cdot 2\pi r = m\angle C \cdot r$.

Using radians, $\frac{l\widehat{AB}}{R} = m\angle C$ and $\frac{l\widehat{DE}}{r} = m\angle C$, so $\frac{l\widehat{AB}}{R} = \frac{l\widehat{DE}}{r}$. The lengths of the arcs are proportional to the lengths of the radii.

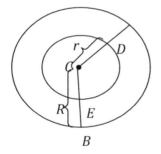

Problem 2
Use similarity to define radian measure of a central angle as the constant of proportionality.

Consider two concentric circles, $\odot C$ with radius r and $\odot C$ with radius R. $\angle ACB$ cuts an arc $(\widehat{AB})$ in the larger circle and a similar arc $(\widehat{DE})$ in the smaller circle. The lengths of the arcs are proportional to the lengths of the radii: $\frac{l\widehat{AB}}{R} = \frac{l\widehat{DE}}{r}$.

$l\widehat{AB} = \frac{m\angle C}{2\pi} \cdot 2\pi R = m\angle C \cdot R \ \rightarrow \ \frac{l\widehat{AB}}{R} = m\angle C$.

$l\widehat{DE} = \frac{m\angle C}{2\pi} \cdot 2\pi r = m\angle C \cdot r \ \rightarrow \ \frac{l\widehat{DE}}{r} = m\angle C$.

Looking at the equations, $\frac{l\widehat{AB}}{R} = m\angle C$ and $\frac{l\widehat{DE}}{r} = m\angle C$, so the constant of the proportion is the radian measure of angle C.

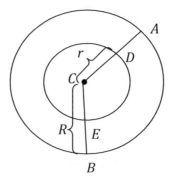

Problem 3

Explain how to find the sum of the interior angles of a polygon, and the measure of one interior angle of a regular polygon.

To find the sum of the interior angles of a polygon, use the formula: sum of interior angles $= (n - 2)180°$, where n is the number of sides in the polygon. This formula works with all polygons, not just regular polygons.

To find the measure of one interior angle of a regular polygon, use the formula $\frac{(n-2)180°}{n}$, where n is the number of sides in the polygon.

Area and perimeter

Triangles

The area of a triangle is given by the formula $A = \frac{1}{2}bh$, where A is the area of the triangle, b is the length of the base, and h is the height of the triangle perpendicular to the base.

If you know the three sides of a scalene triangle, you can use the formula $A = \sqrt{s(s - a)(s - b)(s - c)}$, where A is the area, s is the semiperimeter $s = \frac{a+b+c}{2}$, and a, b, and c are the lengths of the three sides.

The perimeter of a triangle is given by the formula $P = a + b + c$, where P is the perimeter, and a, b, and c are the lengths of the three sides. In this case, the triangle may be any shape. The variables a, b, and c are not exclusive to right triangles in the perimeter formula.

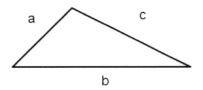

Equilateral triangle: The area of an equilateral triangle is found by the formula $A = \frac{\sqrt{3}}{4}s^2$, where A is the area and s is the length of a side. You could use the $30° - 60° - 90°$ ratios to find the height of the triangle and then use the standard triangle area formula, but this is faster.

The perimeter of an equilateral triangle is found by the formula $P = 3s$, where P is the perimeter and s is the length of a side.

If you know the length of the apothem (distance from the center of the triangle perpendicular to the base) and the length of a side, you can use the formula $A = \frac{1}{2}ap$, where a is the length of the apothem and p is the perimeter.

Isosceles triangle: The area of an isosceles triangle is found by the formula, $A = \frac{1}{2}b\sqrt{a^2 - \frac{b^2}{4}}$, where A is the area, b is the base (the unique side), and a is the length of one of the two congruent sides.

If you do not remember this formula, you can use the Pythagorean Theorem to find the height so you can use the standard formula for the area of a triangle.

The perimeter of an isosceles triangle is found by the formula $A = 2a + b$, where P is the perimeter, a is the length of one of the congruent sides, and b is

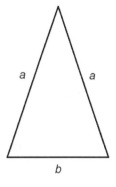

the base (the unique side).

Squares
The area of a square is found by using the formula $A = s^2$, where A is the area of the square, and s is the length of one side. The perimeter of a square is found by using the formula $P = 4s$, where P is the perimeter of the square, and s is the length of one side. Because all four sides are equal in a square, it is faster to multiply the length of one side by 4 than to add the same number four times. You could use the formulas for rectangles and get the same answer.

Rectangles
The area of a rectangle is found by the formula $A = lw$, where A is the area of the rectangle, l is the length (usually considered to be the longer side) and w is the width (usually considered to be the shorter side). The numbers for l and w are interchangeable.
The perimeter of a rectangle is found by the formula $P = 2l + 2w$ or $P = 2(l + w)$, where P is the perimeter of the rectangle, l is the length, and w is the width. It may be easier to add the length and width first and then double the result, as in the second formula.

Parallelograms
The area of a parallelogram is found by the formula $A = bh$, where A is the area, b is the length of the base, and h is the height. Note that the base and height correspond to the length and width in a rectangle, so this formula would apply to rectangles as well.
The perimeter of a parallelogram is found by the formula $P = 2a + 2b$ or $P = 2(a + b)$, where P is the perimeter, and a and b are the lengths of the two sides.
Do not confuse the height of a parallelogram with the length of the second side. The two are only the same measure in the case of a rectangle.

<u>Trapezoids</u>

The area of a trapezoid is found by the formula $A = \frac{1}{2}h(b_1 + b_2)$, where A is the area, h is the height (segment joining and perpendicular to the parallel bases), and b_1 and b_2 are the two parallel sides (bases). Do not use one of the other two sides as the height unless that side is also perpendicular to the parallel bases.

The perimeter of a trapezoid is found by the formula $P = a + b_1 + c + b_2$, where P is the perimeter, and a, b_1, c, and b_2 are the four sides of the trapezoid. Notice that the height does not appear in this formula.

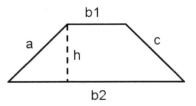

Area, circumference, and diameter of a circle

The area of a circle is found by the formula $A = \pi r^2$, where A is the area and r is the length of the radius. If the diameter of the circle is given, remember to divide it in half to get the length of the radius before proceeding.

The circumference of a circle is found by the formula $C = 2\pi r$, where C is the circumference and r is the radius. Again, remember to convert the diameter if you are given that measure rather than the radius.

To find the diameter when you are given the radius, double the length of the radius.

Lateral surface area and volume of spheres

The lateral surface area is the area around the outside of the sphere. The lateral surface area is given by the formula $A = 4\pi r^2$, where r is the radius. The answer is generally given in terms of pi. A sphere does not have separate formulas for lateral surface area and total surface area as other solid figures do. Often, a problem may ask for the surface area of a sphere. Use the above formula for all problems involving the surface area of a sphere.

The volume is given by the formula $V = \frac{4}{3}\pi r^3$, where r is the radius.

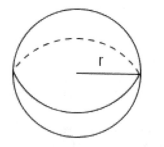

Volume and total surface area of right prisms

The volume of a right prism is found by the formula $V = Bh$, where V is the volume, B is the area of the base, and h is the height (perpendicular distance between the bases).

The total surface area is the area of the entire outside surface of a solid. The total surface area of a right prism is found by the formula $TA = 2B + $ (sum of the areas of the sides), where TA is the total surface area and B is the area of one base. To use this formula, you must remember the formulas for the planar figures.

If the problem asks for the lateral surface area (the area around the sides, not including the bases), use the formula $LA = $ sum of the areas of the sides. Again, you will need to remember the formulas for the various planar figures.

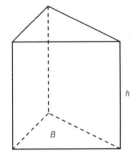

Volume and total surface area of rectangular prisms

The volume of a rectangular prism is found by the formula $V = lwh$, where V is the volume, l is the length, w is the width, and h is the height.

Total surface area is the area of the entire outside surface of the solid. The total surface area of a rectangular prism is found by the formula $TA = 2lw + 2lh + 2wh$ or $TA = 2(lw + lh + wh)$, where TA is the total surface area, l is the length, w is the width, and h is the height.

If the problem asks for lateral surface area, find the total area of the sides, but not the bases. Use the formula $LA = 2lh + 2wh$ or $LA = 2(lh + wh)$, where l is the length, w is the width, and h is the height.

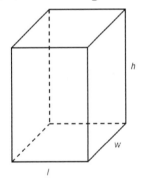

Volume and total surface area of cubes

The volume of a cube is found by the formula $V = s^3$, where V is the volume and s is the length of a side. This is the same as the formula for the volume of a rectangular prism, except the length, width, and height are all equal.

The total surface area of a cube is found by the formula $TA = 6s^2$, where TA is the total surface area and s is the length of a side. You could use the formula for the total surface area of a rectangular prism, but if you remember that all six sides of a cube are equal, this formula is much faster.

Volume, lateral surface area, and total surface area of right circular cylinders

The volume of a right circular cylinder is found by the formula $V = \pi r^2 h$, where V is the volume, r is the radius, and h is the height.

The lateral surface area is the surface area without the bases. The formula is $LA = 2\pi rh$, where LA is the lateral surface area, r is the radius, and h is the height. Remember that if you unroll a cylinder, the piece around the middle is a rectangle. The length of a side of the rectangle is equal to the circumference of the circular base, or $2\pi r$. Substitute this formula for the length, and substitute the height of the cylinder for the width in the formula for the area of a rectangle.

The total surface area of a cylinder is the lateral surface area plus the area of the two bases. The bases of a cylinder are circles, making the formula for the total surface area of a right circular cylinder $TA = 2\pi rh + 2\pi r^2$, where TA is the total area, r is the radius, and h is the height.

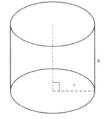

Volume of pyramids

The volume of a pyramid is found by the formula $V = \frac{1}{3}Bh$, where V is the volume, B is the area of the base, and h is the height (segment from the vertex perpendicular to the base). Notice this formula is the same as $\frac{1}{3}$ the volume of a right prism. In this formula, B represents the *area* of the base, not the length or width of the base. The base can be different shapes, so you must remember the various formulas for the areas of plane figures. In determining the height of the pyramid, use the perpendicular distance from the vertex to the base, not the slant height of one of the sides.

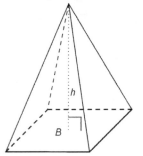

Volume, lateral surface area, and total surface area of right circular cones

The volume of a right circular cone is found by the formula $V = \frac{1}{3}\pi r^2 h$, where V is the volume, r is the radius, and h is the height. Notice this is the same as $\frac{1}{3}$ the volume of a right circular cylinder.

The lateral surface area of a right circular cone is found by the formula $LA = \pi r \sqrt{r^2 + h^2}$ or $LA = \pi r s$, where LA is the lateral surface area, r is the radius, h is the height, and s is the slant height (distance from the vertex to the edge of the circular base). $s = \sqrt{r^2 + h^2}$
The total surface area of a right circular cone is the same as the lateral surface area plus the area of the circular base. The formula for total surface area is $TA = \pi r \sqrt{r^2 + h^2} + \pi r^2$ or $TA = \pi r s + \pi r^2$, where TA is the total surface area, r is the radius, h is the height, and s is the slant height.

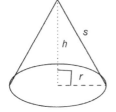

Geometric shapes to model objects

1. The human torso can be modeled using a cylinder. The torso is round with a flat top (shoulders) and a flat bottom (hips).
2. The human head can be modeled using a sphere. The head is round in all directions.
3. A coffee mug can be modeled using a smaller cylinder inside a larger cylinder, aligned at the top. A coffee mug is round with a flat top and bottom.
4. An iPod can be modeled using a shallow rectangular prism. An iPod has two large, flat, rectangular sides (front and back) and four small, rectangular sides (top, bottom, left and right).
5. A book can be modeled on a rectangular prism. A book has six rectangular sides.
6. A tire can be modeled using a smaller cylinder inside a larger cylinder, centered. A tire is round with two flat sides.
7. An apple can be modeled using a sphere. An apple is a round orb.
8. A piece of string cheese can be modeled using a cylinder. A piece of string cheese is round with two flat ends.
9. A log can be modeled using a cylinder. A log is round with two flat ends.

Example problems

Problem 1
The following table lists the four states with the largest populations in 2010 and the area (in square miles) of each state. Find the population density of each and list the states from highest to lowest population density.

State	Population	Area (square miles)
California	37,253,956	158,648
Texas	25,145,561	266,874
New York	19,378,102	49,112
Florida	18,801,310	58,681

California:
$\frac{37{,}253{,}956}{158{,}648} \approx 235$ people/sq. mi
Texas:

$$\frac{25{,}145{,}561}{266{,}874} \approx 94 \text{ people/sq. mi}$$

New York:
$$\frac{19{,}378{,}102}{49{,}112} \approx 395 \text{ people/sq. mi}$$

Florida:
$$\frac{18{,}801{,}310}{58{,}681} \approx 320 \text{ people/sq. mi}$$

Highest to lowest population density: New York, Florida, California, Texas

Problem 2

The following table lists the four states with the smallest populations in 2010 and the area (in square miles) of each state. Find the population density of each and list the states from highest to lowest population density.

State	Population	Area (square miles)
Alaska	710,231	587,878
North Dakota	672,591	70,704
Vermont	625,741	9,615
Wyoming	563,626	97,818

Alaska:
$$\frac{710{,}231}{587{,}878} \approx 1 \text{ person/sq. mi}$$

North Dakota:
$$\frac{672{,}591}{70{,}704} \approx 10 \text{ people/sq. mi}$$

Vermont:
$$\frac{625{,}741}{9{,}615} \approx 65 \text{ people/sq. mi}$$

Wyoming:
$$\frac{563{,}626}{97{,}818} \approx 6 \text{ people/sq. mi}$$

Highest to lowest population density: Vermont, North Dakota, Wyoming, Alaska

Problem 3

Salvador needs to determine if a medallion is made of pure gold. He knows the density of gold is 19.3 g/cm^3 and that the medallion weighs 250 g. Salvador submerges the medallion in a cylindrical container of water with a radius of 3 cm. Determine how many centimeters the water would rise if the medallion were pure gold.

Let x = the volume of a 250 g gold medallion
$$\frac{19.3 \ g}{1 \ cm^3} = \frac{250 \ g}{x \ cm^3}$$
$$19.3 \cdot x = 250 \cdot 1$$
$$x = \frac{250}{19.3}$$

- 72 -

$$x = 12.95$$

A 250 g gold medallion would have a volume of 12.95 cm^3 and would therefore displace 12.95 cm^3 of water.

Define h as the change in height of water after medallion added
$$V = \pi r^2 h$$
$$12.95 = \pi \cdot 3^2 \cdot h$$
$$12.95 = 9\pi \cdot h$$
$$0.46 = h$$
The water will rise 0.46 cm if the medallion is made of pure gold.

Problem 4

A lump of metal, part nickel and part copper, weighs 1000 g. Valerie knows the ratio of nickel to copper is $2 : 3$. The density of nickel is 8.89 g/cm^3, and the density of copper is 8.97 g/cm^3. Determine how many centimeters the water will rise when Valerie places the lump into a square prism container of water with sides 6 cm long.

Nickel

Weight: $\frac{2}{5} \cdot 1000 \text{ g} = 400 \text{ g}$

Displacement: $400 \text{ g} \cdot \frac{1 \text{ cm}^3}{8.89 \text{ g}} = 44.99 \text{ cm}^3$

Copper

Weight: $\frac{3}{5} \cdot 1000 \text{ g} = 600 \text{ g}$

Displacement: $600 \text{ g} \cdot \frac{1 \text{ cm}^3}{8.97 \text{ g}} = 66.89 \text{ cm}^3$

Total Displacement: $44.99 \text{ cm}^3 + 66.89 \text{ cm}^3 = 111.88 \text{ cm}^3$
$$V_s = s^2 \cdot h$$
$$111.88 = 6^2 \cdot h$$
$$111.88 = 36 \cdot h$$
$$3.108 = h$$
The water level will rise 3.108 cm.

Problem 5

A factory cuts large sheets of cardstock (100 in by 102 in) into cards (3 in by 5 in). Determine the maximum number of cards the factory can cut and which side of the cards should be cut from the 100 in side of the sheets.

Area of the large sheet: $A_{sheet} = l \cdot w = 100 \cdot 102 = 10{,}200 \ in^2$
Area of one card: $A_{card} = l \cdot w = 3 \cdot 5 = 15 \ in^2$
Number of cards made: $\frac{10200}{15} = 680$

Option 1: 3 in side cut from 100 in side
$\frac{100}{3} = 33.3333 \rightarrow 99 \ in$ used and 33 cards per side
$\frac{102}{5} = 20.4 \rightarrow 100 \ in$ used and 20 cards per side
$33 \cdot 20 = 660$ cards total

Option 2: 5 *in* side cut from the 100 *in* side

$\frac{100}{5} = 20 \rightarrow 100$ *in* used and 20 cards per side

$\frac{102}{3} = 34 \rightarrow 102$ *in* used and 34 cards per side

$34 \cdot 20 = 680$ cards total

Option 2 should be used to achieve the maximum number of cards made and avoid any wasted material.

<u>Problem 6</u>
A display box is designed to hold a single baseball so the ball touches all six faces of the box. If the diameter of a baseball is 2.9 in, how much empty space is in the box around the ball.

The volume of the empty space can be calculated by subtracting the volume of the ball from the volume of the cube-shaped box.

$$V_{box} = s^3 = 2.9^3 = 24.389$$
$$V_{ball} = \frac{4}{3} \cdot \pi r^3 = \frac{4}{3} \cdot \pi \cdot (1.45)^3 = 12.77$$
$$V_{space} = V_{box} - V_{ball} = 24.389 - 12.77 = 11.619$$

The box has 11.619 cubic inches of space around the baseball.

Volume of a prism, cylinder, pyramid, and cone

The formula for a prism or a cylinder is $V = Bh$, where B is the area of the base and h is the height of the solid. For a cylinder, the area of the circular base is determined by the formula $B = \pi r^2$. For a prism, the area of the base depends on the shape of the base; for example, a triangular base would have area $\frac{1}{2}bh$, while a rectangular base would have area bh. For a pyramid or cone, the volume is $V = \frac{1}{3}Bh$, where B once again is the area of the base and h is the height. In other words, the volume of a pyramid or cone is one-third the volume of a prism or cylinder with the same base and the same height.

Example problems

<u>Problem 1</u>
A takeout container is in the shape of an inverted truncated pyramid, with a rectangular top measuring 6 by 9 inches and a rectangular bottom measuring 4 by 6 inches; the container is 3 inches high. What is the container's volume?

To find the volume of a truncated pyramid—a pyramid with a smaller pyramid cut off from it—we must find the volumes of the larger and smaller pyramids. To do this, we must find their heights.

The larger pyramid's base is 1.5 times as long and 1.5 times as wide as the smaller pyramid's. The cross-sections of the two pyramids are triangles that are similar to each other, so the larger one must be 1.5 times the height of the smaller. The height of the truncated pyramid (which is the difference in height between the larger and smaller pyramids) is 3 inches, so we have two

- 74 -

equations: $H = 1.5h$ and $H = h + 3$, where H is the height of the larger pyramid and h is the height of the smaller pyramid. Solving this system gives us $H = 9$ and $h = 6$.

So the larger pyramid, with the 9- by 6-inch base, has a height of 9 inches and therefore a volume of $9 \times 6 \times 9 \div 3 = 162$ in³. The smaller pyramid has a volume of $6 \times 4 \times 6 \div 3 = 48$ in³, so their difference (the volume of the container) is 114 in³.

Problem 2
Describe the relationship between the number of faces, edges, and vertices of a polyhedron. How many vertices does a rhombic triacontahedron (a 30-sided polyhedron whose faces are all rhombuses) have?

The number of faces, edges, and vertices of a polyhedron follows Euler's formula: $V + F = E + 2$, where V, F, and E are the number of vertices, the number of faces, and the number of edges, respectively. A rhombic triacontahedron has 30 faces, and since each face has four edges and each edge is shared by exactly two faces, there must be a total of $4 \times 30 \div 2 = 60$ edges. Plugging these numbers into Euler's formula, we get $V + 30 = 60 + 2$, or $V = 32$.

Problem 3
If the radius of a cylinder is doubled, what happens to its volume? If the height is doubled instead, what happens to the volume?

The volume of a cylinder is proportional to the square of the radius; therefore, if the radius is doubled, the volume is quadrupled. To put it algebraically, the original volume is $\pi r^2 h$, where r is the radius and h is the height; replacing r with $2r$ yields $\pi(2r)^2 h$, or $4\pi r^2 h$, which is four times the original volume.

The volume is also directly proportional to the height; if the height is doubled, the volume is doubled as well. To put it algebraically, since the original volume is $\pi r^2 h$, replacing h with $2h$ yields $\pi r^2(2h)$, or $2\pi r^2 h$, which is twice the original volume.

Problem 4
One sphere has four times the surface area of another. What is the ratio of their volumes? If the smaller sphere has a radius of 3 feet, what is the volume of the larger sphere?

The surface area of a sphere is proportional to the square of its radius, and the volume is proportional to the cube of the radius. This means that for a sphere's surface area to increase by a factor of 4, its radius only needs to increase by a factor of $\sqrt{4}$, or 2. If the larger sphere has twice the radius of the smaller, then its volume must be 2^3, or 8, times greater. The ratio of the spheres' volumes is thus 8:1.

If the smaller sphere's radius is 3 feet, the larger sphere's radius is 6 feet, so its volume is $\frac{4}{3}\pi r^3$, or 288π ft³.

Example problems

Problem 1

What is the area of a regular octagon of side length 8?

Possibly the easiest way to determine the area of a regular octagon is to think of it as a square with truncated corners—in other words, a square minus four isosceles right triangles. The hypotenuses of the triangles make the "diagonal" sides of the octagon, so they measure 8 units each and their legs measure $4\sqrt{2}$ units each. Therefore, the sides of the large square containing the octagon measure $8 + 8\sqrt{2}$ units each.

The large square, then, has area $(8 + 8\sqrt{2})^2$ or $192 + 128\sqrt{2}$ units². The triangles each have area 16 units², so the total area of all four of them is 64 units². So, the total area of the octagon is $192 + 128\sqrt{2} - 64 = 128 + 128\sqrt{2}$ units².

Problem 2

A pizza with an 18-inch diameter is cut into 12 equal slices. What is the area of each slice? How many linear inches of crust does each one have? What is the total perimeter of each slice?

Each slice represents a twelfth of the pizza, both in area and perimeter of crust.

The radius of the pizza is 9 inches, so the area of the whole pizza is 81π in²; therefore, the area of each slice is $\frac{81}{12}\pi$, or $\frac{27}{4}\pi$, in².
The circumference of the pizza is 18π inches, so each slice has a twelfth of that circumference, which is 1.5π inches of crust.
The total perimeter of each slice is the length of the crust plus the length of the two cuts to the center. The cuts are each 9 inches long, so the total perimeter of each slice is $1.5\pi + 18$ inches.

Problem 3

In how many of the following cases are two triangles guaranteed to be congruent?
A. All 3 sides are congruent (SSS)
B. All 3 angles are congruent (AAA)
C. 2 sides and angle between are congruent (SAS)
D. 2 angles and 1 side are congruent (ASA or AAS)
E. 2 sides and non-included angle are congruent (SSA)
For each case where the triangles are not guaranteed to be congruent, explain why not.

A. When all three sides are congruent (SSS), the triangles are congruent.
B. When all three angles are congruent (AAA), the triangles are similar, but not necessarily congruent.

C. When two sides and the angle between them are congruent (SAS), the triangles are congruent.

D. When any two angles are congruent (ASA or AAS), the third angle must also be congruent, because the sum of all three angles is always 180°. Therefore, the triangles must be similar; hence, if they also have one corresponding side that is congruent, then all the sides must be congruent.

E. When two sides and the non-included angle are congruent (SSA), the triangles are generally not congruent; there are two different triangles that could be constructed with those two sides and that angle. However, if the angle is a right angle, then the triangles are congruent.

Problem 4

Are two isosceles triangles congruent if they have the same base? Are two isosceles triangles congruent if they have the same vertex angle?

Two isosceles triangles with the same base are not necessarily congruent, because their legs can be of any length. For example, one triangle might have side lengths 3, 5, and 5, and another might have side lengths 3, 6, and 6.

However, when we know the vertex angle of an isosceles triangle, we also know what the base angles must be. Since all three angles must add up to 180°, once we subtract the measure of the vertex angle from 180° we know that the other two angles must each measure half of what's left. Therefore, when two isosceles triangles have the same vertex angle, their base angles must also be the same, and the triangles are similar. If the two triangles have the same vertex angle and the same base, then they are congruent based on the AAS or ASA theorem.

Problem 5

Are two right triangles congruent if they have the same leg lengths? Are two right triangles congruent if they have the same hypotenuse?

Two right triangles with the same leg lengths must also, by the Pythagorean theorem, have the same hypotenuse. Therefore, all three of their side lengths must be the same, and so the two triangles must be congruent.

However, the reverse is not necessarily true. Two right triangles can have the same hypotenuse but have different leg lengths; for example, one triangle with a hypotenuse of length 25 could have legs of lengths 7 and 24 and another could have legs of lengths 15 and 20. With only one side length in common, those two triangles would not be congruent.

Problem 6

A tall window is in the shape of a rectangle with a half-circle attached:

If the window is three feet wide, and its total height is five and a half feet, what is its area to the nearest square inch?

> Since the window is three feet wide, the radius of the semicircular portion is 18 inches, or one and a half feet. If the total height of the window is five and a half feet, that means the rectangular portion is 4 feet tall.

> Converting to inches, the rectangular portion of the window is 48 by 36 inches, so its area is 1728 square inches. The semicircular portion has an area of ½ $\pi(18)^2$, or 162π, square inches, which is approximately 509 in². The total area of the window is therefore approximately 1728 + 509 = 2237 in².

Problem 7

A stone obelisk has the shape of a square prism with a pyramid on top. The height of the prism is 40 feet, the height of the pyramid is 4 feet, and the width of both is 6 feet. What is the total surface area of the obelisk, not counting the base?

> The surface area of the prism just consists of the areas of the four vertical faces. Each of these faces is 6 by 40 feet, so each face's area is 240 ft²

> The total area of the four rectangular faces is 960 ft².

> The surface area of the pyramid just consists of the areas of the four triangular faces. The slant height of each face is the hypotenuse of the triangle that forms a cross-section of half the pyramid, with one leg equal to half the base (3 feet) and another leg equal to the height (4 feet). So the slant height of each face is 5 feet, and the area of each face is half the base times the slant height, or 15 ft². All four faces therefore total 60 ft², and combined with the rectangular faces, the total surface area is 1020 ft².

Problem 8

A right triangle with leg lengths 10 and 24 is inscribed in a semicircle, with its hypotenuse as the circle's diameter. What is the area of the semicircle excluding the triangle?

> 10-24-26 is a multiple of the Pythagorean triple 5-12-13, but even without knowing this, we can use the Pythagorean theorem to calculate that the hypotenuse of the triangle, and thus the diameter of the semicircle, is 26 units. Therefore, the radius of the semicircle is 13 units, and so its area is half the area of the corresponding circle, or $0.5\pi \times 13^2 = 84.5\pi$ units².

> The area of the triangle, meanwhile, is $0.5 \times 10 \times 24 = 120$ units², so the area of the semicircle excluding the triangle is $84.5\pi - 120$ units². This cannot be simplified unless we use a decimal approximation: 84.5π is approximately 265.5, making the area of the semicircle minus the triangle approximately 145.5 units².

Problem 9

A circular archery target is four feet across and divided into ten concentric rings of equal width; that is, the innermost circle has a radius of 2.4 inches and each of the other nine rings has a width of 2.4 inches. If an arrow hits the target in a random location, what is the probability that it will hit the innermost ring? What is the probability that it will hit the outermost ring?

The radius of the whole target is 24 inches; therefore the area of the whole target is $24^2\pi$ in², or 576π in². The radius of the innermost ring is 2.4 inches, so its area is 5.76π in². The innermost ring has $\frac{1}{100}$ the area of the whole target, so there is a 1% chance the arrow will hit it.

To find the area of the outermost ring, we must subtract the area of the rest of the target from the area of the whole target. The rest of the target, not including the outermost ring, is a circle with radius 21.6 inches, so its area is 466.56π in². The outermost ring therefore has area $576\pi - 466.56\pi = 109.44\pi$ in². 109.44π divided by 576π is 0.19, so there is a 19% chance the arrow will hit the outer ring.

This problem can also be solved in a simpler way. Since the inner circle has $\frac{1}{10}$ the radius of the whole target, we know it has $\frac{1}{100}$ the area because area is proportional to the square of the radius. Similarly, the circle excluding the outer ring has $\frac{9}{10}$ the radius of the whole target, so it has $\frac{81}{100}$ the area, and the outer ring therefore has $\frac{19}{100}$ the area.

Problem 10

Given a line l and a point P in the same plane, how many lines through P can be drawn in the plane that are perpendicular to l?

Only one line can be drawn through P that is perpendicular to l. To prove this, first suppose P lies on l. Many different lines can be drawn through P, but each of those lines will make a different angle with l. There is exactly one line that will make a 90° angle with l, hence exactly one line perpendicular to l.

Next, suppose P doesn't lie on l. Many different lines can be drawn that connect P to different points on l. Suppose A and B are separate points on l, and suppose the lines PA and PB are both perpendicular to l. This means that triangle PAB has two right angles: angle PAB and angle PBA. However, it's impossible for a triangle to have two 90° angles, because all three of its angles can't sum to more than 180. Therefore, there cannot be two such separate points A and B; there can be only one point on l through which a perpendicular line can be drawn to P.

Problem 11

Given a circle and a point P outside the circle, how many lines can be drawn through P that are tangent to the circle? What if P lies on the circle? What if it is inside?

Exactly two tangent lines can be drawn to a circle from an exterior point. The farther away the point is from the circle, the farther apart the two points of tangency are along the circle, and the smaller the angle between the two tangent lines. As P gets closer to the circle, the two points of tangency get

- 79 -

Copyright © Mometrix Media. You have been licensed one copy of this document for personal use only. Any other reproduction or redistribution is strictly prohibited. All rights reserved.

closer together; when *P* is no longer external but lies directly on the circle, then the two points of tangency become one point, which is also *P*, and there is only one tangent line through that point.

If *P* is inside the circle, however, no tangent lines at all can be drawn through it. Any line passing through *P* would have to pass through the circle twice, once on each side of *P*; therefore, it would not be a tangent line.

Problem 12

Quadrilateral *ABCD*, whose vertices are located at *A*(4, 4), *B*(6.5, 3), *C*(5, -1.5),and *D*(-3, 2), is translated a certain distance across the plane to form quadrilateral *A'B'C'D'*. If point *A'* is at (1.5, 2), what are the coordinates of points *B'*, *C'*, and *D'*?

> In a translation, all the points in a figure are moved exactly the same distance in the same direction; in other words, they are moved the same horizontal distance and the same vertical distance. Point *A'* is 2.5 units left and 2 units down from point *A*; therefore, all three of the other vertices must also be translated 2.5 units left and 2 units down from their original places. Therefore, Point *B'* is at (4, 1); point *C'* is at (2.5, -3.5); and point *D'* is at (-5.5, 0).

Problem 13

Points *A*, *B*, *C*, and *D* have coordinates (2, 3), (-1, 5), (-2, -2), and (4, -3), respectively. If quadrilateral *ABCD* is rotated 90° counterclockwise about the origin to create quadrilateral *A'B'C'D'*, what are the coordinates of *A'*, *B'*, *C'*, and *D'*?

> When a point is rotated counterclockwise about the origin, it is now as far above or below the origin as it was previously right or left (respectively) of the origin, and as far left or right of the origin as it was above or below the origin. In other words, its old *x*-coordinate is its new *y*-coordinate, and its old *y*-coordinate is the negative of its new *x*-coordinate.
>
> Therefore, the points *A*(2, 3), *B*(-1, 5), *C*(-2, -2), and *D*(4, -3) map to the points *A'*(-3, 2), *B'*(-5, -1), *C'*(2, -2), and *D'*(3, 4).

Problem 14

Define congruence of two figures in terms of rigid motion.

> Two figures are congruent if one figure can be made to carry onto the second figure using one or more rotations, reflections, and/or translations

Problem 15

Describe "corresponding parts of congruent triangles are congruent" using the definition of congruence in terms of rigid motion.

> Two triangles are congruent in terms of rigid motion when one triangle is the image of the other triangle. In one triangle, each side and angle is matched with only one side or angle of the other triangle. If a series of rigid motions align the two triangles, then the sides that are the same and the angles that are the same will be matched. If the sides and angles are all

- 80 -

matched, then the congruent triangles have six congruent parts. Thus, the parts that correspond after transformation are congruent with each other.

Problem 16
Use the definition of congruence in terms of rigid motion to describe the criteria for angle-side-angle (ASA) congruence for triangles.

A figure is congruent to another figure if one can be superimposed on the other by rigid motion (translation, reflection, rotation). When two congruent triangles are superimposed, it two angles and the side between the two angles align, the other two sides and angle will also align, Therefore, it is sufficient to show when proving two triangles congruent that two angles and the side between the angles are the same.

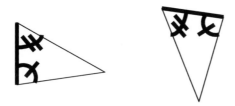

Problem 17
Use the definition of congruence in terms of rigid motion to describe the criteria for side-angle-side (SAS) congruence for triangles.

A figure is congruent to another figure if one can be superimposed on the other by rigid motion (translation, reflection, rotation). When two congruent triangles are superimposed, it two sides and the angle between the two angles align, the other side and two angles will also align, Therefore, it is sufficient to show when proving two triangles congruent that two sides and the angle between the sides are the same.

Problem 18
Use the definition of congruence in terms of rigid motion to describe the criteria for side-side-side (SSS) congruence for triangles.

A figure is congruent to another figure if one can be superimposed on the other by rigid motion (translation, reflection, rotation). When two congruent triangles are superimposed, if all three sides align, the three angles will also align, therefore, it is sufficient to show when proving two triangles congruent that the measures of the three sides of the one triangle are equal to the measures of the three sides of the other.

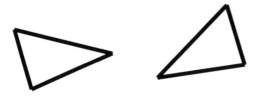

Problem 19
Show that vertical angles are congruent.

Draw two lines which intersect at a point. This point of intersection becomes a shared vertex of four angles created by the intersection of the two lines. Vertical angles are across from each other, and there are two pairs of vertical angles formed by the intersection of two lines. When one angle is rotated about the point of intersection by 180°, it aligns with its vertical angle. Therefore, the two angles are congruent.

Problem 20
Show that when two parallel lines are cut by a transversal, the resulting alternate interior angles are congruent.

Draw two lines which intersect at a point. This point of intersection becomes a shared vertex of four angles created by the intersection of the two lines. Vertical angles are across from each other, and there are two pairs of vertical angles formed by the intersection of two lines. When one angle is rotated about the point of intersection by 180°, it aligns with its vertical angle. Therefore, the two angles are congruent.

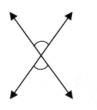

Problem 21
Show that when two parallel lines are cut by a transversal, the resulting corresponding angles are congruent.

Draw two parallel lines cut by a transversal and note two corresponding angles. Translate one parallel line along the transversal until it aligns with the other parallel line. The two noted angles align and are therefore congruent.

Problem 22
Show the measures of the interior angles of a triangle add to 180°.

Draw a line on a piece of paper. Cut each of the sides of the triangle at the midpoint to create three angles. Transform the three angles using rotation to align all three so their vertices are at the same point. Two of the angles' sides are parallel to the line, and the third angle's sides touch the other sides of the angles. Because the three angles come together to form a line, which measures 180°, the three angles add to 180°.

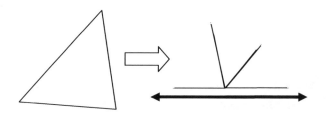

Problem 23
Show the base angles of an isosceles triangle are congruent.

Draw an isosceles triangle. Reflect one side of the triangle across the perpendicular bisector of the base. The two base angles align and are therefore congruent.

Problem 24
Show that the three medians of a triangle meet at a point.

Draw a triangle. From each vertex, draw a line to the midpoint of the opposite side. These three medians intersect at one point in the triangle. Show that this is true for acute, right, and obtuse triangles.

Problem 25
Show that the segment which joins the midpoints of two sides of a triangle is parallel to the third side and half its length.

Draw a triangle and construct a line segment which connects the midpoints of two sides of the triangle. Translate the line segment so that it aligns with the third side and one endpoint of the segment is aligned with the endpoint of the third side. Since the line segment was able to be translated without rotation, it is parallel to the third side of the triangle.
Draw a line that is perpendicular to the third side of the triangle through the translated segment's endpoint which does not lie on the triangle's vertex. Reflect the line segment across this line. The endpoint that was aligned with the first vertex is now aligned with the second vertex; thus, the line segment is half the length of the third side of the triangle.

Problem 26
Show that opposite sides of parallelograms are congruent. Show that opposite angles of parallelograms are congruent.

Draw a parallelogram.
Translate one side of the parallelogram along the adjacent sides until it is aligned with the opposite side. The endpoints align, so the sides are congruent.
Use the point where the diagonals intersect as a point of rotation. Rotate the parallelogram 180° so that the angles are aligned with the angles opposite them.

Problem 27
Show that the diagonals of parallelograms bisect each other.

> Draw a parallelogram and its two diagonals. Use one diagonal as a line of
> reflection. Reflect the other diagonal onto itself. Since the endpoints align,
> the line of reflection is a bisector of the reflected diagonal. Repeat the
> process for the other diagonal.

Problem 28
Show that a rectangle is a parallelogram with congruent diagonals.

> A rectangle is a parallelogram with four right angles. Draw a rectangle and
> its two diagonals. Find the midpoints of two opposite sides of the rectangle
> and connect them to construct a line of reflection. Reflect one of the right
> triangles over the line of reflection. The reflected triangle's hypotenuse,
> which is the one of the rectangle's diagonals, aligns with another triangle's
> hypotenuse, which is the rectangle's other diagonal. Thus, the diagonals are
> congruent, so a rectangle is a parallelogram with congruent diagonals.

Dilation

Example problems
Problem 1: Verify that a dilation takes a line not passing through the center of the dilation to
a parallel line, and leaves a line passing through the center unchanged.

> $\overleftrightarrow{AB}$ is a line that does not pass through the center of the dilation. When line
> segment $\overline{AB}$ is dilated using a scale factor of 2, line segment $\overline{A'B'}$ is created.
> Translate the intersection of $\overleftrightarrow{AB}$ and the line through A and the center of
> dilation to the intersection of $\overleftrightarrow{A'B'}$ and the line through A and the center of
> dilation. Since $\overleftrightarrow{AB}$ overlaps $\overleftrightarrow{A'B'}$, the two lines are parallel.
> $\overleftrightarrow{CD}$ is a line that passes through the center of the dilation. When line segment
> $\overline{CD}$ is dilated using a scale factor of 2, $\overline{C'D'}$ is created. Both lines $\overleftrightarrow{CD}$ and $\overleftrightarrow{C'D'}$
> are the same line which passes through the center of dilation, so the dilation
> left the line unchanged.

Problem 2: Verify that a dilation of a line segment is longer or shorter than the original line
segment in the ratio given by the scale factor.

> $\overline{AB}$ is a line segment that is dilated using a scale factor of ½. Translate $\overline{AB}$
> along one line through the center of dilation until A is aligned with A'. Since
> the ratio is less than 1, $\overline{AB}$ is larger than $\overline{A'B'}$, so using the perpendicular
> bisector of $\overline{AB}$ as a line of reflection, reflect $\overline{A'B'}$ so that A' is now aligned
> with B. Since B' did not move, and is still at the point of intersection between
> $\overline{AB}$ and the perpendicular bisector, the ratio of $\overline{A'B'}$ to $\overline{AB}$ is 1 to 2.
> $\overline{CD}$ is a line segment that is dilated using a scale factor of 2. Translate $\overline{CD}$
> along one line through the center of dilation until C is aligned with C'. Since
> the ratio is greater than 1, $\overline{C'D'}$ is larger than $\overline{CD}$, so using the perpendicular

bisector of $\overline{C'D'}$ as a line of reflection, reflect $\overline{CD}$ so that C is now aligned with D'. Since D did not move, and is still at the point of intersection between $\overline{C'D'}$ and the perpendicular bisector, the ratio of $\overline{C'D'}$ to $\overline{CD}$ is 2 to 1.

Proving similarity

<u>Example problems</u>
Problem 1: Use transformations and the definition of similarity to prove that two figures are similar.

The corresponding angles of similar figures are congruent, and the corresponding sides are proportional. Rotate and translate one figure onto the other so that one pair of corresponding angles aligns. Continue to translate the figure so that corresponding angles are aligned, one pair of angles at a time. After verifying that all pairs of corresponding angles are congruent, determine if the sides are proportional. Position the figures so that corresponding sides are parallel and so that the smaller figure does not overlap the larger figure. Use a straightedge to draw lines that will connect each pair of corresponding vertices. Extend the lines to find a point of possible intersection. If all the lines meet at a single point, that point is the center of dilation and the two figures are similar.

Problem 2: Use transformations and the definition of similarity to show two triangles are similar if all corresponding pairs of angles are congruent and all corresponding pairs of sides are proportional.

Rotate and translate one triangle so that one pair of corresponding angles aligns. Continue to translate the triangle so that corresponding angles are aligned, one pair of angles at a time. After verifying that all pairs of corresponding angles are congruent, determine if the sides are proportional. Position the triangles so that corresponding sides are parallel and so that the smaller triangle does not overlap the larger. Use a straightedge to draw lines that will connect each pair of corresponding vertices. Extend the lines to find a point of possible intersection. If all the lines meet at a single point, that point is the center of dilation and the two figures are similar.

Problem 3: Use the properties of similarity transformations to describe the criteria for angle-angle (AA) similarity of triangles.

When a triangle is dilated (a similarity transformation) the lengths of its side change, but its angle measures remain the same. When an angle of a triangle is aligned with the corresponding angle of a dilated triangle, the two angles match; the same is true for the other two pairs of corresponding angles. When the corresponding angles of two triangles are congruent, the two triangles are similar. It is sufficient, however, to show that two of the three pairs of corresponding angles are congruent to determine the triangles' similarity: the third pair of corresponding angles must also be congruent since the sum of the angles in each triangle is 180°.

Line dividing a triangle proportionally

<u>Example problems</u>
Problem 1: Prove that a line which passes through a triangle and which is parallel to one of its sides divides the other two sides proportionally.

In the diagram, PQ is parallel to BC. When two parallel lines are cut by a transversal, corresponding angles are congruent. So, $\angle APQ \cong \angle PBC$ and , $\angle AQP \cong \angle QCB$. Thus, by the AA similarity theorem, $\triangle ABC$ is similar to $\triangle APQ$. The ratios of corresponding sides of similar triangles are proportional, so $\frac{AB}{AP} = \frac{AC}{AQ}$. Since $AB = AP + PB$ and $AC = AQ + QC$, $\frac{AP+PB}{AP} = \frac{AQ+QC}{AQ}$. This can be rewritten as $\frac{AP}{AP} + \frac{PB}{AP} = \frac{AQ}{AQ} + \frac{QC}{AQ} \rightarrow 1 + \frac{PB}{AP} = 1 + \frac{QC}{AQ} \rightarrow \frac{PB}{AP} = \frac{QC}{AQ}$. Therefore, a line which passes through a triangle and which is parallel to one of its sides divides the other two sides proportionally.

Problem 2: Prove a line that divides two sides of a triangle proportionally is parallel to the third side.

If line PQ divides $\triangle ABC$ proportionally, then $\frac{PB}{AP} = \frac{QC}{AQ}$.

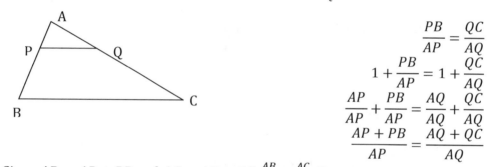

$$\frac{PB}{AP} = \frac{QC}{AQ}$$
$$1 + \frac{PB}{AP} = 1 + \frac{QC}{AQ}$$
$$\frac{AP}{AP} + \frac{PB}{AP} = \frac{AQ}{AQ} + \frac{QC}{AQ}$$
$$\frac{AP + PB}{AP} = \frac{AQ + QC}{AQ}$$

Since $AB = AP + PB$ and $AC = AQ + QC$, $\frac{AB}{AP} = \frac{AC}{AQ}$. Since $\angle BAC$ is shared with $\triangle ABC$ and $\triangle APQ$, and since the two sides flanking the angle are proportional, by SAS similarity, $\triangle ABC$ is similar to $\triangle APQ$. Corresponding angles of similar triangles are congruent, so $\angle APQ \cong \angle PBC$ and , $\angle AQP \cong \angle QCB$. When two lines, such as PQ and BC, are cut by a transversal, such as AB, and corresponding angles, such as so $\angle APQ$ and $\angle PBC$ are congruent, the two lines are parallel. So, PQ is parallel to BC. Therefore, a line that divides two sides of a triangle proportionally is parallel to the third side.

Proving the Pythagorean Theorem

To prove the Pythagorean Theorem for right $\triangle ABC$, show $(AB)^2 + (BC)^2 = (AC)^2$. Identify three similar triangles created by drawing altitude $\overline{BD}$. Use rotation and translation to verify that the three triangles are similar by AA. $\triangle ABC \sim \triangle BDC \sim \triangle ADB$. Similar triangles have proportional sides, so $\frac{AB}{AD} = \frac{AC}{AB}$ and $\frac{BC}{DC} = \frac{AC}{BC}$. Also note, $AD + DC = AC$.

Use cross multiplication:	$\dfrac{AB}{AD} = \dfrac{AC}{AB} \rightarrow (AB)^2 = (AD)(AC)$ $\dfrac{BC}{DC} = \dfrac{AC}{BC} \rightarrow (BC)^2 = (DC)(AC)$
Add these two new equations together:	$(AB)^2 + (BC)^2 = (AD)(AC) + (DC)(AC).$
Use the distributive property to simplify the right side:	$(AB)^2 + (BC)^2 = (AD + DC)(AC)$
Use substitution:	$(AB)^2 + (BC)^2 = (AC)(AC)$
Simplify:	$(AB)^2 + (BC)^2 = (AC)^2$

(drawings not to scale)

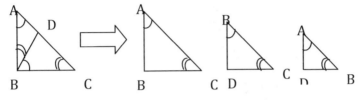

Triangle congruence (ASA)

Triangle congruence (ASA) can be used to solve problems involving triangles when two pairs of corresponding angles are known to be congruent and the contained sides are also congruent. To solve for the third angle, subtract the sum of the known angles from 180°. Once triangle congruence is established, all other corresponding parts of the triangles can also be identified as congruent.

Example problem
Problem 1: Given $\triangle ABC$ and $\triangle DEF$. Show $\triangle ABC \cong \triangle DEF$.

Since $m\angle A = m\angle D = 75°$, $AB = DE = 15$, and $m\angle B = m\angle E = 30°$, $\triangle ABC \cong \triangle DEF$ by Angle-Side-Angle Congruence.

Problem 2: Given $\triangle ABC$ and $\triangle DEF$. Find the length of AC.

Since corresponding parts of congruent triangles are congruent, $AC = DF = 7.76$.

Problem 3: Given $\triangle ABC$ and $\triangle DEF$. Find the measure of $\angle F$.

Since the sum of the angles in a triangle is 180°, add the measure of $\angle D$ and the measure of $\angle E$ and subtract from 180°: $180° - (75° + 30°) = 180° - 105° = 75°$. $m\angle F = 75°$.

Triangle congruence (SAS)

Triangle congruence (SAS) can be used to solve problems involving triangles when two pairs of corresponding sides are known to be congruent and the contained angles are also congruent. Once triangle congruence is established, all other corresponding parts of the triangles can also be identified as congruent.

<u>Example problems</u>
Problem 1: Given △ ABC and △ EDC. Show △ $ABC \cong$ △ EDC.

Since $BC = DC = 21$, $\angle BCA \cong \angle DCE$ (vertical angles), and $AC = EC = 19.22$, △ $ABC \cong$ △ DEF by Side-Angle-Side Congruence.

Problem 2: Given △ ABC and △ EDC. Find the length of AB.

Since Corresponding Parts of Congruent Triangles are Congruent, $AB = ED = 11.55$.

Problem 3: Given △ ABC and △ EDC. Find the measure of $\angle E$.

The sum of the angles in a triangle is 180°.
$$\angle C + \angle D + \angle E = 180°$$
$$33° + 65° + \angle E = 180°$$
$$98° + \angle E = 180°$$
$$\angle E = 82°$$

Triangle congruence (SSS)

Triangle congruence (SSS) can be used to solve problems involving triangles when all pairs of corresponding sides are known to be congruent. Once triangle congruence is established, all other corresponding parts of the triangles can also be identified as congruent.

<u>Example problems</u>
Problem 1: Given △ ABC and △ DEF, Show △ $ABC \cong$ △ DEF.

Since $AB = DE = 8.66$, $BC = EF = 5$, and $AC = DF = 10$, △ $ABC \cong$ △ DEF by Side-Side-Side Congruence.

Problem 2: Given △ ABC and △ DEF, Find the measure of $\angle D$, $\angle E$, and $\angle F$.

Since the sum of the angles in a triangle add to 180°, write an equation for each triangle.

△ ABC:	△ DEF:
$(2y + 4) + (14x - 8) + (3x + 39) = 180$ $17x + 2y + 35 = 180$ $17x + 2y = 145$ $y = \dfrac{145 - 17x}{2}$	$(5x - 5) + (5y - 5) + (7y - 1) = 180$ $5x + 12y - 11 = 180$ $5x + 12y = 191$

Solve the system of equations.

$5x + 12\left(\dfrac{145 - 17x}{2}\right) = 191$ $5x + 870 - 102x = 191$ $-97x = -679$ $x = 7$	$y = \dfrac{145 - 17(7)}{2}$ $y = \dfrac{145 - 119}{2} = \dfrac{26}{2}$ $y = 13$

$$m\angle D = 5x - 5 = 5(7) - 5 = 35 - 5 = 30°$$

$$m\angle E = 7y - 1 = 7(13) - 1 = 91 - 1 = 90°$$
$$m\angle F = 5y - 5 = 5(13) - 5 = 65 - 5 = 60°$$

Triangle similarity (AA)

Triangle similarity (AA) can be used to solve problems involving triangles when two pairs of corresponding angles are known to be congruent. To solve for the third angle, subtract the sum of the known angles from 180°. Once triangle similarity is established, all pairs of corresponding angles in the triangles can be identified as congruent and all pairs of corresponding sides in the triangles can be identified as proportional.

Example problems
Problem 1: Given $\triangle ABC$ and $\triangle DEF$, Find the measure of $\angle E$. Find the measure of $\angle C$.

1. Since the sum of the angles of a triangle is 180°, $m\angle E = 180° - (29.9° + 56.3°) = 180° - 86.2° = 93.8°$.
2. Since the sum of the angles of a triangle is 180°, $m\angle C = 180° - (56.3° + 93.8°) = 180° - 150.1° = 29.9°$.

Problem 2: Given $\triangle ABC$ and $\triangle DEF$, Show $\triangle ABC \sim \triangle DEF$. Find the length of DE. Find the length of BC.

1. Since $m\angle A = m\angle D = 56.3°$ and $m\angle B = m\angle E = 93.8°$, $\triangle ABC \sim \triangle DEF$ by Angle-Angle Similarity.
2. Since corresponding sides are proportional in similar triangles, $\frac{AB}{DE} = \frac{AC}{DF}$.
   $\frac{3}{DE} = \frac{6}{18} \rightarrow 54 = 6 \cdot DE \rightarrow DE = 9$.
3. Since corresponding sides are proportional in similar triangles, $\frac{BC}{EF} = \frac{AC}{DF}$.
   $\frac{BC}{15} = \frac{6}{18} \rightarrow 18 \cdot BC = 90 \rightarrow BC = 5$.

Problem 3: Given $\triangle ABC$, $\triangle DEF$, and $\triangle GHI$, Solve for the length of the hypotenuse in $\triangle ABC$. Solve for the length of DE in $\triangle DEF$. Solve for the measure of $\angle G$ in $\triangle GHI$.

1. In $\triangle ABC$, AC is the hypotenuse and $\sin A = \frac{BC}{AC}$. So, $\sin 60 = \frac{15}{AC} \rightarrow AC = \frac{15}{\sin 60} = 17.32$.
2. In $\triangle DEF$, $\sin F = \frac{DE}{DF}$. So, $\sin 45 = \frac{DE}{16} \rightarrow DE = 16 \cdot \sin 45 = 11.31$.
3. In $\triangle GHI$, $\sin G = \frac{HI}{GI}$. So, $\sin G = \frac{21}{28} \rightarrow G = \sin^{-1}\frac{21}{28} = 48.59°$.

Cosine to solve problems involving right triangles

Problems that can be solved using cosine must give specific information and ask for a specific solution.

Given	Unknown
one acute angle and the side adjacent to that angle	the hypotenuse
one acute angle and the hypotenuse	the side adjacent to that angle
the hypotenuse and one side	the angle adjacent to the known side **to solve this problem, use $\cos^{-1}$**

Example problems

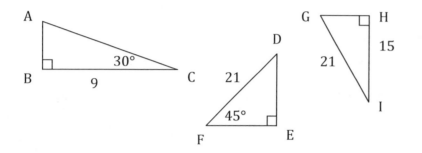

Given $\triangle ABC$, $\triangle DEF$, and $\triangle GHI$,

1. Solve for the length of the hypotenuse in $\triangle ABC$.

2. Solve for the length of EF in $\triangle DEF$.

3. Solve for the measure of $\angle I$ in $\triangle GHI$.

1. In $\triangle ABC$, AC is the hypotenuse and $\cos C = \frac{BC}{AC}$. So, $\cos 30 = \frac{9}{AC} \rightarrow AC = \frac{9}{\cos 30} = 10.39$.

2. In $\triangle DEF$, $\cos F = \frac{EF}{DF}$. So, $\cos 45 = \frac{EF}{21} \rightarrow EF = 21 \cdot \cos 45 = 14.85$.

3. In $\triangle GHI$, $\cos I = \frac{HI}{GI}$. So, $\cos I = \frac{15}{21} \rightarrow I = \cos^{-1} \frac{15}{21} = 44.42°$.

Tangent to solve problems involving right triangles

Problems that can be solved using tangent must give specific information and ask for a specific solution.

Given	Unknown
one acute angle and the side opposite that angle	the side adjacent to that angle
one acute angle and the side adjacent to that angle	the side opposite that angle
two legs	either of the two acute angles **to solve this problem, use $\tan^{-1}$**

Example problems

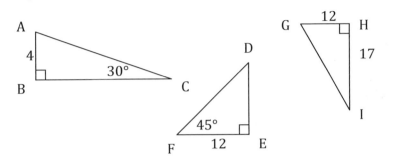

Given △ ABC, △ DEF, and △ GHI,

1. Solve for the length of BC in $\triangle ABC$.

2. Solve for the length of DE in $\triangle DEF$.

3. Solve for the measure of $\angle I$ in $\triangle GHI$.

1. In $\triangle ABC$, $\tan C = \frac{AB}{BC}$. So, $\tan 30 = \frac{4}{BC} \rightarrow BC = \frac{4}{\tan 30} = 6.93$.

2. In $\triangle DEF$, $\tan F = \frac{DE}{EF}$. So, $\tan 45 = \frac{DE}{12} \rightarrow DE = 12 \cdot \tan 45 = 12$.

3. In $\triangle GHI$, $\tan I = \frac{GH}{HI}$. So, $\tan I = \frac{12}{17} \rightarrow I = \tan^{-1}\frac{12}{17} = 35.22°$.

Pythagorean Theorem to solve problems involving right triangles

Problems that can be solved using the Pythagorean Theorem must give specific information and ask for a specific solution.

Given	Unknown
two legs	the hypotenuse
one leg and the hypotenuse	the other leg

Example problems

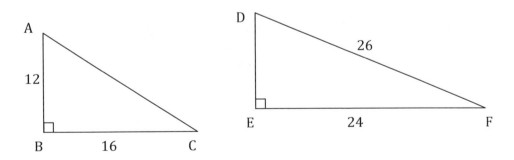

Given △ ABC and △ DEF,

1. Solve for the length of AC in $\triangle ABC$.
2. Solve for the length of DE in $\triangle DEF$.

1. In $\triangle ABC$, $AB^2 + BC^2 = AC^2$. So, $12^2 + 16^2 = AC^2 \rightarrow AC^2 = 144 + 256 = 400 \rightarrow AC = \sqrt{400} = 20$.

2. In $\triangle DEF$, $DE^2 + EF^2 = DF^2$. So, $DE^2 + 24^2 = 26^2 \rightarrow DE^2 + 576 = 676 \rightarrow DE^2 = 676 - 576 = 100 \rightarrow DE = \sqrt{100} = 10$

Formula $Area_{\triangle ABC} = \frac{1}{2} \cdot a \cdot b \cdot \sin C$

Example problem

From the triangle area formula $Area = \frac{1}{2}bh$, where b is the length of triangle's base, and h is the triangle's height; derive the formula $Area_{\triangle ABC} = \frac{1}{2} \cdot a \cdot b \cdot \sin C$ by drawing an auxiliary line from a vertex perpendicular to the opposite side.

$Area_{\triangle ABC} = \frac{1}{2} \cdot b \cdot h$. Notice that h is an auxiliary line from the vertex, B, and perpendicular to the opposite side, AC, and h divides $\triangle ABC$ into two right triangles. From the triangle on the right, $\sin C = \frac{h}{a}$, so $h = a \cdot \sin C$. Substituting this into the area formula creates $Area_{\triangle ABC} = \frac{1}{2} \cdot b \cdot (a \cdot \sin C)$, which can be written $Area_{\triangle ABC} = \frac{1}{2} \cdot a \cdot b \cdot \sin C$.

Equilateral, isosceles, and scalene triangles

An equilateral triangle is a triangle with three congruent sides. An equilateral triangle will also have three congruent angles.
An isosceles triangle is a triangle with two congruent sides. An isosceles triangle will also have two congruent angles opposite the two congruent sides.
A scalene triangle is a triangle with no congruent sides. A scalene triangle will also have three angles of different measures. The angle with the largest measure is opposite the longest side, and the angle with the smallest measure is opposite the shortest side.

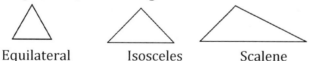

Equilateral   Isosceles   Scalene

Acute, right, and obtuse triangles and sum of the angles of a triangle

An acute triangle is a triangle whose three angles are all less than 90°. If two of the angles are equal, the acute triangle is also an isosceles triangle. If the three angles are all equal, the acute triangle is also an equilateral triangle.
A right triangle is a triangle with exactly one angle equal to 90°. All right triangles follow the Pythagorean Theorem. A right triangle can never be acute or obtuse.
An obtuse triangle is a triangle with exactly one angle greater than 90°. The other two angles may or may not be equal. If the two remaining angles are equal, the obtuse triangle is also an isosceles triangle.

The sum of the measures of the interior angles of a triangle is always 180°. Therefore, a triangle can never have more than one angle greater than or equal to 90°.

Triangle Inequality Theorem

The Triangle Inequality Theorem states that the sum of the measures of any two sides of a triangle is always greater than the measure of the third side. If the sum of the measures of two sides were equal to the third side, a triangle would be impossible because the two sides would lie flat across the third side and there would be no vertex. If the sum of the measures of two of the sides was less than the third side, a closed figure would be impossible because the two shortest sides would never meet.

Altitude, height, concurrent, and orthocenter

Altitude of a Triangle: A line segment drawn from one vertex perpendicular to the opposite side. In the diagram below, $\overline{BE}$, $\overline{AD}$, and $\overline{CF}$ are altitudes.
Height of a Triangle: The length of the altitude, although the two terms are often used interchangeably.
Concurrent: Lines that intersect at one point. In a triangle, the three altitudes are concurrent.
Orthocenter of a Triangle: The point of concurrency of the altitudes of a triangle. Note that in an obtuse triangle, the orthocenter will be outside the circle, and in a right triangle, the orthocenter is the vertex of the right angle.

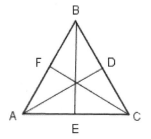

Median and centroid

Median of a Triangle: A line segment drawn from one vertex to the midpoint of the opposite side. This is not the same as the altitude, except the altitude to the base of an isosceles triangle and all three altitudes of an equilateral triangle.
Centroid of a Triangle: The point of concurrency of the medians of a triangle. This is the same point as the orthocenter only in an equilateral triangle. Unlike the orthocenter, the centroid is always inside the triangle. The centroid can also be considered the exact center of the triangle. Any shape triangle can be perfectly balanced on a tip placed at the centroid. The centroid is also the point that is two-thirds the distance from the vertex to the opposite side.

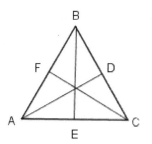

Perpendicular bisectors and angle bisectors

Perpendicular bisector: A line that bisects the side of a triangle at a right angle. The perpendicular bisectors of a triangle are concurrent at a point called the circumcenter that is equidistant from the three vertices. The circumcenter is also the center of the circle that can be circumscribed about the triangle.

Angle bisector: A line that divides the vertex angle of a triangle into two equal parts. The angle bisectors are concurrent at a point called the incenter that is equidistant from the three sides. The incenter is also the center of the largest circle that can be inscribed in the triangle.

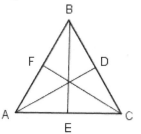

Similar triangles and relationships between sides and angles and midpoints and sides

Similar triangles are triangles whose corresponding angles are equal and whose corresponding sides are proportional. Represented by AA. Similar triangles whose corresponding sides are congruent are also congruent triangles.

In any triangle, the angles opposite congruent sides are congruent, and the sides opposite congruent angles are congruent. The largest angle is always opposite the longest side, and the smallest angle is always opposite the shortest side.

The line segment that joins the midpoints of any two sides of a triangle is always parallel to the third side and exactly half the length of the third side.

Congruent triangles

Three sides of one triangle are congruent to the three corresponding sides of the second triangle. Represented as SSS.

Two sides and the included angle (the angle formed by those two sides) of one triangle are congruent to the corresponding two sides and included angle of the second triangle. Represented by SAS.

Two angles and the included side (the side that joins the two angles) of one triangle are congruent to the corresponding two angles and included side of the second triangle. Represented by ASA.

Two angles and a non-included side of one triangle are congruent to the corresponding two angles and non-included side of the second triangle. Represented by AAS.

Note that AAA is not a form for congruent triangles. This would say that the three angles are congruent, but says nothing about the sides. This meets the requirements for similar triangles, but not congruent triangles.

Leg, hypotenuse, and Pythagorean Theorem

A right triangle has exactly one right angle. (If a figure has more than one right angle, it must have more than three sides, since the sum of the three angles of a triangle must equal 180°.)

The side opposite the right angle is called the hypotenuse. The other two sides are called the legs.

The Pythagorean Theorem states a unique relationship among the legs and hypotenuse of a right triangle: $a^2 + b^2 = c^2$, where a and b are the lengths of the legs of a right triangle, and c is the length of the hypotenuse. Note that this formula will only work with right triangles. Do not attempt to use it with triangles that are not right triangles.

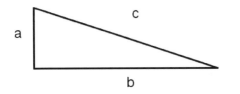

Practice Test #1

Practice Questions

1. What mathematician is generally considered the father of geometry?

Ⓐ Descartes

Ⓑ Euclid

Ⓒ Plato

Ⓓ Gauss

2. What postulate of Euclidean geometry distinguishes it from non-Euclidean geometry?

Ⓐ The parallel postulate

Ⓑ The right angle postulate

Ⓒ Koch's postulate

Ⓓ Euclid's third postulate

3. Which statement must be false in Euclidean geometry but can be true in non-Euclidean geometry?

Ⓐ Parallel lines never intersect

Ⓑ A circle is a two-dimensional figure

Ⓒ A quadrilateral has four sides of equal length

Ⓓ The sum of the angles in a triangle is less than $180°$

4. Write the converse of the statement "If a bird is a penguin, then it cannot fly".

Ⓐ "If a bird is not a penguin, then it can fly"

Ⓑ "If a bird is not a penguin, then it cannot fly"

Ⓒ "If a bird can fly, then it is not a penguin"

Ⓓ "If a bird cannot fly, then it is a penguin"

5. Which statement is logically equivalent to "If John is 10 years old, then he is in the fifth grade"?

Ⓐ "If John is not 10 years old, then he is not in the fifth grade"

Ⓑ "If John is in the fifth grade, then he is 10 years old"

Ⓒ "If John is not in the fifth grade, then he is not 10 years old"

Ⓓ All of the above

6. Which of the following is a counterexample for the statement "If today is the weekend, then it is Saturday"?

Ⓐ It is before 6 pm on Saturday

Ⓑ Today is Sunday

Ⓒ Tomorrow is Sunday

Ⓓ It is Monday morning

7. Find a counterexample for the statement "All prime numbers are odd".

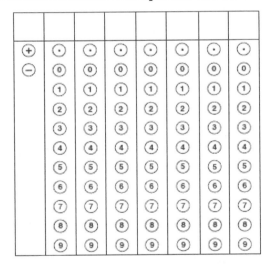

8. After seeing a list of the first 20 prime numbers, Tim conjectured that the difference between any two consecutive prime numbers is always less than 10. Which type of reasoning did he use?

Ⓐ Indirect reasoning

Ⓑ Deductive reasoning

Ⓒ Inductive reasoning

Ⓓ Circular reasoning

9. Use inductive reasoning to formulate a conjecture about the difference between the squares of consecutive positive integers.

Ⓐ The differences are positive odd numbers

Ⓑ The differences are prime numbers

Ⓒ The differences are perfect squares

Ⓓ The differences are divisible by positive prime numbers

10. Triangle *ABC* is isosceles. Every isosceles triangle has two congruent angles. What type of reasoning allows us to therefore conclude that triangle *ABC* has two congruent angles?

Ⓐ Deductive reasoning

Ⓑ Indirect reasoning

Ⓒ Inductive reasoning

Ⓓ Circular reasoning

11. The sum of the angles of a triangle is 180°. For a quadrilateral, the sum is 360°. In general, adding an additional side to a polygon adds 180° to the sum of the angles. Use this pattern to write an algebraic expression for the sum of the angles of a polygon with *n* sides.

Ⓐ 120*n*-180

Ⓑ 120(*n*-2)

Ⓒ 180*n*-180

Ⓓ 180(*n*-2)

12. Using the variable *n*, write an algebraic expression for the number of squares in the figure below.

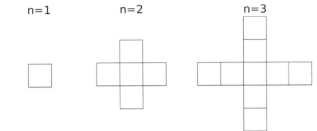

Ⓐ 4*n*

Ⓑ 4*n*-3

Ⓒ 5*n*

Ⓓ 5*n*-4

13. An equilateral triangle whose side is 2 feet long has an area of $\sqrt{3}$ square feet. When the side length is increased to 4 feet, the area becomes $4\sqrt{3}$ square feet. And when it is 8 feet, the area is $16\sqrt{3}$ square feet. Make a generalization about the relationship between the side length of an equilateral triangle and its area.

Ⓐ The area of an equilateral triangle is always $\sqrt{3}$ times the side length

Ⓑ The ratio of the side length and the area is in the proportion 2: $\sqrt{3}$

Ⓒ When the side length doubles, the area quadruples

Ⓓ When the side length increases by 2, the area increases by $3\sqrt{3}$

14. What transformation is represented by the figure below?

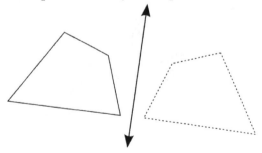

Ⓐ A translation

Ⓑ A rotation

Ⓒ A dilation

Ⓓ A reflection

15. Which triangle is a right triangle?

16. In a right triangle, the length of one leg is 15/17 of the length of the hypotenuse. What fraction of the length of the hypotenuse is the length of the other leg?

Ⓐ 1/17

Ⓑ 2/17

Ⓒ 2/15

Ⓓ 8/17

17. In a 30-60-90 triangle, the lengths of two sides are 4 and 8. What is the length of the third side?

Ⓐ 4

Ⓑ 6

Ⓒ $4\sqrt{2}$

Ⓓ $4\sqrt{3}$

18. To make wooden triangular supports for a wall, 5 in. by 5 in. squares are cut in half by cutting from one corner to the opposite corner. What is length of the hypotenuse of the resulting triangular support in inches? Round to the nearest inch.

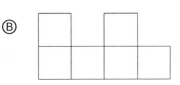

19. Besides a single point, what shape can the intersection of a plane and a sphere be?

Ⓐ A cone

Ⓑ A circle

Ⓒ A triangle

Ⓓ An ellipse

20. Which of the following is a net of a cube?

Ⓐ  Ⓑ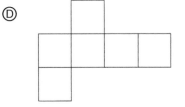

Ⓒ Ⓓ

21. Which graph represents the triangle with vertices at (-1,2), (3,8), and (7,4)?

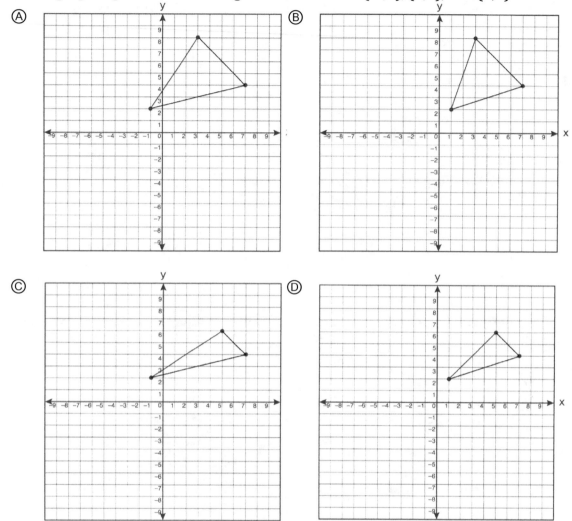

22. What kinds of lines have undefined slopes?

Ⓐ Parallel lines

Ⓑ Vertical lines

Ⓒ Horizontal lines

Ⓓ None of the above

23. Which line appears to have a slope of 2?

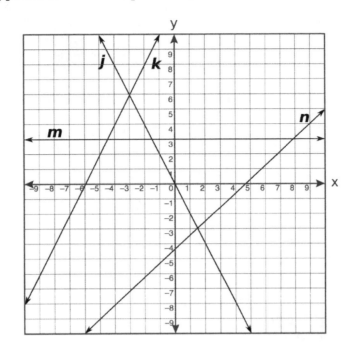

Ⓐ Line *j*

Ⓑ Line *k*

Ⓒ Line *m*

Ⓓ Line *n*

24. The slope of a line, *AB*, containing *A* (3,-1) and *B* (6,*k*) is 2. What is the value of *k*?

Ⓐ -7

Ⓑ -5/2

Ⓒ 1/2

Ⓓ 5

25. The equation of line *L* is $y = 2x - 3$. Find an equation of the line that is perpendicular to *L* and intersects it at (2, 3).

Ⓐ $y = -\frac{1}{2}x + 1$

Ⓑ $y = -\frac{1}{2}x + 4$

Ⓒ $y = \frac{1}{2}x + 1$

Ⓓ $y = \frac{1}{2}x + 4$

26. **What is the slope of the line that contains A (-5, 3) and B (-1, -4)?**

   (A) -1/4

   (B) -7/4

   (C) -1/6

   (D) 7/6

27. **What is the midpoint of the line segment with endpoints at A (5, 2) and B (-1, 6)?**

   (A) (2, 2)

   (B) (3, 2)

   (C) (2, 4)

   (D) (3, 4)

28. **The midpoint between two points, A and B, is M (3, 6). If the coordinates of B are (0, 2), what is length of line AB?**

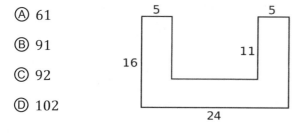

29. **In the figure, all angles are right angles. Calculate its perimeter of the figure.**

   (A) 61

   (B) 91

   (C) 92

   (D) 102

30. An architect plans to build a circular pathway around a fountain that has a radius of 20 feet. The pathway will be made of concrete and be 5 feet wide. What will be the area of the pathway when it is complete? Round your answer to the nearest square foot.

Ⓐ 707 square feet

Ⓑ 867 square feet.

Ⓒ 1209 square feet

Ⓓ 1901 square feet

31. The radius of the circle to the right is 10. Find the area of the shaded sector. Round to the nearest tenth.

Ⓐ 12.2

Ⓑ 19.4

Ⓒ 61.1

Ⓓ 314.5

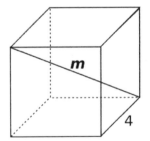

32. A circle is divided into 15 congruent sectors. What is the arc length of each sector?

Ⓐ 2°

Ⓑ 15°

Ⓒ 20°

Ⓓ 24°

33. The cube in the figure to the right has sides of length 4. Find the length of line *m*, which travels from one corner of a cube to the opposite corner.

Ⓐ $4\sqrt{2}$

Ⓑ $4\sqrt{3}$

Ⓒ 8

Ⓓ $8\sqrt{2}$

34. What is the surface area of a right cylinder with a diameter of 5 and a height of 8? Round to the nearest whole number.

Ⓐ 165

Ⓑ 283

Ⓒ 330

Ⓓ 408

35. The Great Pyramid of Giza is a regular square pyramid roughly 450 feet tall and 750 feet long on each side. Assuming it is a regular square pyramid, what is its volume?

Ⓐ 112,500 cubic feet

Ⓑ 337,500 cubic feet

Ⓒ 84,375,000 cubic feet

Ⓓ 253,125,000 cubic feet

36. In the dartboard to the right, the radius of the smaller circle is 6 in. and the radius of the larger one is 12 in. If a dart is thrown at the dartboard, what is the probability that it hits somewhere in the section marked by the X?

Ⓐ 1/16

Ⓑ 1/8

Ⓒ 3/32

Ⓓ 3/16

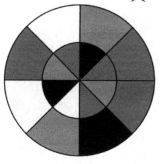

37. A builder wants to cut a one-foot board into segments that are 3 cm long. How many full segments can he cut?

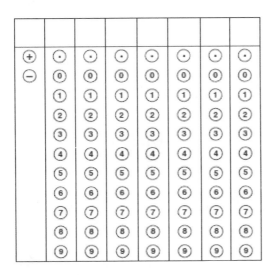

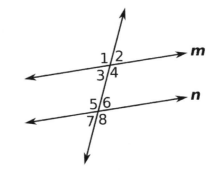

38. In the figure to the right, line *m* is parallel to line *n*. Which angle must be congruent to angle *1*?

Ⓐ Angle *2*

Ⓑ Angle *6*

Ⓒ Angle *7*

Ⓓ Angle *8*

39. What is the sum of the measures of the interior angles of an octagon?

Ⓐ 540°

Ⓑ 1080°

Ⓒ 1440°

Ⓓ 2160°

40. In a circle with center *C*, line *AB* is a tangent and line *BC* is a radius. Which of the following must be true of *AB* and *BC*?

Ⓐ They are the same length

Ⓑ They are perpendicular

Ⓒ They are parallel

Ⓓ They have the same arc length

41. In the figure to the right, *C* is the center of the circle. Calculate the value of *x*.

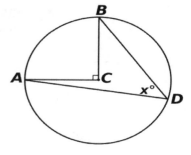

    Ⓐ 45

    Ⓑ 67.5

    Ⓒ 90

    Ⓓ 95

42. Which of the following transformations preserves angle measures?

    Ⓐ Translation

    Ⓑ Rotation

    Ⓒ Reflection

    Ⓓ All of the above

43. In the figure to the right, which postulate most directly allows us to conclude that triangle *ABC* is congruent to *ACD*?

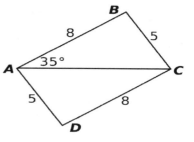

    Ⓐ Postulate SSS

    Ⓑ Postulate SAS

    Ⓒ Postulate ASA

    Ⓓ Postulate AAS

44. In the figure to the right, *CD* is perpendicular to lines *AC* and *BD*. In addition *AC* is congruent to *BD*. Which of the following must also be true?

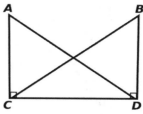

    Ⓐ *AC* is congruent to *CD*

    Ⓑ Angle *A* is congruent to angle *B*

    Ⓒ Triangles *ACD* and *BCD* are isosceles triangles

    Ⓓ Angle *B* is a right angle

45. An artist makes a replica of the *Mona Lisa* for a postcard. To make the replica, he uses 1 inch on the postcard to represent 6 inches in the original. If the original painting is about 30 in. × 21 in., what are the dimensions of the replica?

    Ⓐ 4 in. × 2 in.

    Ⓑ 5 in. × $3\frac{1}{2}$ in.

    Ⓒ 12 in. × $7\frac{1}{2}$ in.

    Ⓓ 24 in. × 15 in.

46. The lengths of the sides of triangle *ABC* are 4, 8, and 9. The lengths of the shortest two sides of similar triangle *DEF* are 10 and 20. What is the length of the longest side of *DEF*?

Ⓐ 41/4

Ⓑ 25/2

Ⓒ 45/2

Ⓓ 45

47. In the figure below, the shaded rectangle *ABED* is similar to the large rectangle *ACFD*. What is the value of *x*?

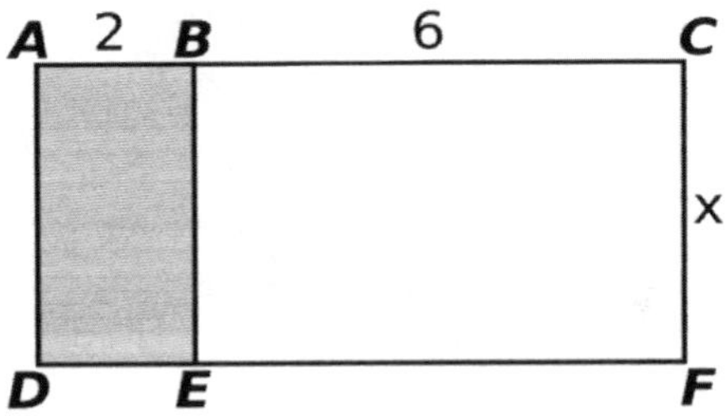

Ⓐ 5/2

Ⓑ 3

Ⓒ 4

Ⓓ 6

48. At a certain time of day, a 10-foot pole casts a 6-foot shadow. How tall is a man who casts a $3\frac{1}{2}$ foot shadow at the same time of day?

Ⓐ 5 ft

Ⓑ 5 ft 3 in

Ⓒ 5 ft 6 in

Ⓓ 5 ft 10 in

49. In the figure to the right, *BD* is parallel to *CE*. Use similar triangles to find the length of *CE*.

Ⓐ 2

Ⓑ 4

Ⓒ 6

Ⓓ 8

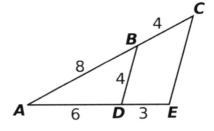

50. The figure to the right contains a right triangle _ABD_ with its altitude drawn. Use the similarity properties of right triangles to find the value of _x_.

Ⓐ 5

Ⓑ 8

Ⓒ 9

Ⓓ 10

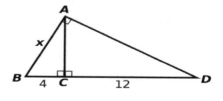

51. The lengths of the sides of a quadrilateral _ABCD_ are 4, 6, 7, and 10. What is the perimeter of similar quadrilateral _EFGH_ if the length of its shortest side is 8?

⊕	⊙	⊙	⊙	⊙	⊙	⊙	⊙
⊖	⓪	⓪	⓪	⓪	⓪	⓪	⓪
	①	①	①	①	①	①	①
	②	②	②	②	②	②	②
	③	③	③	③	③	③	③
	④	④	④	④	④	④	④
	⑤	⑤	⑤	⑤	⑤	⑤	⑤
	⑥	⑥	⑥	⑥	⑥	⑥	⑥
	⑦	⑦	⑦	⑦	⑦	⑦	⑦
	⑧	⑧	⑧	⑧	⑧	⑧	⑧
	⑨	⑨	⑨	⑨	⑨	⑨	⑨

52. To help plan a building, an architect makes a model of it that is 6 inches tall with a total volume of 4 cubic feet. Calculate the volume of the actual building if it will be 20 feet tall.

Ⓐ 160 cubic feet

Ⓑ $\frac{4000}{27}$ cubic feet

Ⓒ 256,000 cubic feet

Ⓓ 512,000 cubic feet

Answers and Explanations

1. B: Euclid, a Greek mathematician who lived around 300 BC, is usually considered the father of geometry and an important figure in the development of the notion of mathematical rigor. His most famous work is *Elements*, a collection of geometric proofs, starting with definitions and axioms and proceeding to more complicated propositions. It was still a widely read work until the 20th century.

2. A: Euclid's famous treatise, *Elements*, contained five postulates. For centuries, it was generally agreed by mathematicians that the first four postulates were self-evident, whereas the fifth postulate, the so-called parallel postulate, was not as obvious because of its length and difficulty. In the nineteenth century, some mathematicians began to explore what would happen if the parallel postulate was assumed to be false. The resulting geometry came to be known as non-Euclidean geometry.

3. D: Non-Euclidean geometry is geometry in which the parallel postulate is assumed to be false. Pictorially, this means that Euclidean geometry is on a flat plane (it is the geometry we are most familiar with), whereas non-Euclidean geometry is on a curved surface. As a result, the angles of a triangle in Euclidean geometry always add up to exactly 180°. On the other hand, in non-Euclidean geometry, the angles can add up to either less than or more than 180° depending on whether the surface is curved like a saddle-shaped plane or an ellipsoid.

4. D: The converse of a statement "If p, then q" is "If q, then p", where p and q are any statement. In other words, to construct the converse, switch the two halves of the conditional. In the given expression, the p-statement is "a bird is a penguin" and the q-statement is "it [a bird] cannot fly". When you switch the two halves, the result is "If a bird cannot fly, then it is a penguin".

5. C: A conditional and its contrapositive always have the same truth table, so they are considered logically equivalent. On the other hand, the inverse and converse do not have the same truth table as the original statement, so they are not considered logically equivalent. Examine the choices A, B, and C and notice that choice A is the inverse of the original statement, choice B is the converse, and choice C is the contrapositive. Therefore, only the statement in choice C is logically equivalent to the original statement.

6. B: A counterexample is a specific example that violates a general statement. Since the given statement "If today is the weekend, then it is Saturday" is a conditional (i.e., it is in the form "If..., then..."), a counterexample will be an example in which the "if" part of the statement is true, but the "then" part is false. Therefore, for this problem, we need to find a day that is part of the weekend but is not Saturday. The only day that fits that description is Sunday.

7. 2: A counterexample is a specific example that violates a general statement. Since the statement is "All prime numbers are odd", a counterexample would be a prime number that is even. The only even prime number is 2 because any even number greater than it is divisible by 2.

8. C: Inductive reasoning involves making an observation, finding a pattern, and making a general conjecture based on that pattern. In this example, the pattern Tim found was that in the first 20 prime numbers, no two consecutive prime numbers are 10 or more apart. Using inductive reasoning, he generalized this pattern of the first 20 primes to apply to all prime numbers.

9. A: Inductive reasoning involves making an observation, finding a pattern, and making a general conjecture based on that pattern. The first four differences are:

$$1^2 - 0^2 = 1 - 0 = 1$$
$$2^2 - 1^2 = 4 - 1 = 3$$
$$3^2 - 2^2 = 9 - 4 = 5$$
$$4^2 - 3^2 = 16 - 9 = 7$$

Notice that these numbers are the first four positive odd numbers. Therefore, using inductive reasoning, we can make the conjecture that the difference between the squares of *any* consecutive positive integers is a positive odd number. Although this type of reasoning is not considered a valid method of mathematical proof, it is still useful for discovering possible theorems that can later be proved rigorously.

10. A: Deductive reasoning asserts conclusion that must necessarily be true based on a set of premises. In this problem, the premises are "Triangle *ABC* is an isosceles" and "Every isosceles triangle has two congruent angles". Since triangle *ABC* is an instance of an isosceles triangle, it must *necessarily* have two congruent angles. Therefore, this is an example of deductive reasoning.

11. D: From the problem, the sum of the angles of a triangle is 180°. So, when $n=3$, the correct algebraic expression will be 180. Plugging in 3 for n into the choices eliminates choices B and C right away since they don't result in 180. In addition, the expression should increase by 180 when n increases by one. This tells us that 180 should be multiplied by n in the algebraic expression. Therefore, the answer must be D. Choice A is incorrect because when n increases by one, the expression increases by 120, not 180.

12. B: Examine the three figures. To organize the information, make a table.

n	# of Squares
1	1
2	5
3	9

Examine the data to find a pattern. Notice that when n increases by one, the number of squares increases by four. This suggests that the coefficient of n should be four in the algebraic expression. Another important observation is that when $n=1$, there is only one square. As a result, leaving the expression as simply $4n$ will not work because $4(1)=4$. Therefore, you need to offset this difference by subtracting three from $4n$ to get $4n-3$. To check the expression, substitute 1, 2, and 3, for n and calculate the result.

13. C: To organize the information, make a table.

Side Length	Area
2	$\sqrt{3}$
4	$4\sqrt{3}$
8	$16\sqrt{3}$

Examine the data to find a pattern. In the side length column, the numbers are doubled from 2 to 4 and then from 4 to 8. In the area column, the numbers quadruple: $4\sqrt{3}$ is four times $\sqrt{3}$ and $16\sqrt{3}$ is four times that. Therefore, the pattern is that when the side length of the equilateral triangle double, the area quadruples.

14. D: A translation is a transformation in which a figure slides to another position but retains its size and orientation. In a rotation, a figure turns about some fixed point. In a dilation, a figure changes its size but retains its position and orientation. In a reflection, a figure flips over a line so that it appears to be backwards (or upside down as the case may be). Notice that in the figure above, the quadrilateral appears to be reflected about the middle line.

15. A: If a triangle is a right triangle, then the lengths of its sides obey the Pythagorean theorem, $a^2 + b^2 = c^2$. To determine which triangle is right, test each triangle by substituting its side lengths into the Pythagorean theorem. Start with the first triangle.

$5^2 + 12^2 =? 13^2$
$25 + 144 =? 169$
$169 = 169$

The first triangle obeys the Pythagorean theorem. Therefore, it is a right triangle. You can check the other three triangles to see that they do not work.

16. D: In this problem, the exact lengths of the sides are neither given nor asked for. Instead, we are dealing with a right triangle in which the proportion of the lengths is fixed. To make the problem easier to work with, it is okay to give the sides of the triangle specific number lengths. Let's use 17 for the length of the hypotenuse.

The length of the leg is 15/17 times the length of the hypotenuse, so it 15. Since this is a right triangle, we can use the Pythagorean theorem to find the missing side.

$a^2 + 15^2 = 17^2$
$a^2 + 225 = 289$
$a^2 = 64$
$a = 8$

Therefore, the missing side is 8. Reread the question again. It asks for a fraction for the length of the leg (8) to the length of the hypotenuse (17). Thus, the answer is 8/17.

17. D: In a 30-60-90 triangle, the ratio of the lengths of the sides are $1: \sqrt{3}: 2$. In other words, the length of the longer leg is $\sqrt{3}$ times the length of the shorter leg, and the hypotenuse is twice the length of the shorter leg. We are already given that two sides are 4 and 8. It may be helpful to draw a triangle as a guide. Since the given lengths are in the ratio 1:2, they must be the shorter leg and the hypotenuse. Therefore, the missing side is the longer leg. To find its length, multiply the length of the shorter leg, 4, by $\sqrt{3}$ to get the answer. The answer is $4\sqrt{3}$.

18. 7: The original pieces of wood are squares with 5 in. sides. Therefore, when the squares are cut in half, the resulting triangle is a 45-45-90 triangle. In 45-45-90 triangle, the ratio of the sides is $1:1:\sqrt{2}$. From the way the squares are cut, we also know that the legs of the triangles are 5 in. long. Thus, to find the length of the hypotenuse, multiply the length of the leg, 5 in., by $\sqrt{2}$ and round to the nearest whole number. The result is 7 in.

19. B: The intersection of two figures in three-dimensional space is the set of points where the two figures meet. If a plane is tangent to a sphere (i.e. if it just barely touches it), then the intersection is a point. Otherwise, the intersection is a circle as shown in the figure below.

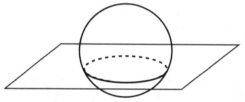

20. D: A net is a two-dimensional figure that can be folded into a three-dimensional solid. Since a cube has six square faces, each of the four choices (A, B, C, and D) has six squares. Examine the four choices one-by-one while imagining folding the nets along their solid lines to get a cube. In choices A, B, and C, there are problems with the nets that make it impossible to get a cube with a bottom and a top face. Only in choice D can you fold the four horizontal squares in the middle to get the sides of the cube and then fold the remaining two squares to get the top and bottom of the cube.

21. A: To graph points on a coordinate axis, start at the origin, (0,0), and move left or right based on the first coordinate (the x-coordinate) and then up or down based on the second coordinate (the y-coordinate. For instance, to graph the first point, (-1,2), start at the origin and move left one unit and up two units, and then put a dot where you end up. After graphing the three points, (-1,2), (3,8), and (7,4), the result is the triangle in the graph in choice A.

22. B: The formula for the slope m of a line containing the points (x_1, y_1) and (x_2, y_2) is $m = \frac{y_2 - y_1}{x_2 - x_1}$. In this formula, the only way the slope can be undefined is if the denominator is zero since division by zero is undefined. The denominator will only be zero when $x_2 = x_1$, or, in other words, when the x-coordinates of the two points are equal. Two points have the same x-coordinates only when they are on the same vertical line. Therefore, only vertical lines have undefined slopes.

23. B: The slope of a line is a number that represents its steepness. Lines with positive slope go from the bottom-left to the top-right, lines with negative slope go from the top-left to the bottom-right, and horizontal lines have zero slope. You can also think of slope as being $\frac{rise}{run}$. In particular, a slope of 2 (which is equivalent to a slope of 2/1) means that the line rises (goes up) 2 units every time it runs (goes to the right) 1 unit. Looking closely at line k, notice that for every 2 units it goes up, it goes to the right 1 unit.

24. D: The formula for the slope m of a line containing the points (x_1, y_1) and (x_2, y_2) is $m = \frac{y_2 - y_1}{x_2 - x_1}$. Substitute the coordinates of the given points, A and B, into the formula and set the slope m equal to 2. Then solve for k.

$$2 = \frac{k - (-1)}{6 - 3}$$
$$2 = \frac{k + 1}{3}$$
$$6 = k + 1$$
$$5 = k$$

Therefore, the value of k is 5.

25. B: The given equation of L is in slope-intercept form $y = mx + b$, where m is the slope of the line and b is the x-intercept. Consequently, we know that the slope of L is 2 and its x-intercept is -3. In addition, every line that is perpendicular to L will have a slope that is the *negative reciprocal* of the slope of L. Since the reciprocal of the slope of L (which is 2) is 1/2, the negative reciprocal is -1/2. So, we now know that the equation for the line perpendicular to L is y=-(1/2)x+b.

To find the y-intercept b, substitute the point (2,3) into the equation $y = -\frac{1}{2}x + b$ and solve for b.

$$3 = -\frac{1}{2}(2) + b$$
$$3 = -1 + b$$
$$4 = b$$

Finally, plug the value of b into the equation. The result is $y = -\frac{1}{2}x + 4$.

26. B: The formula for the slope m of a line containing the points (x_1, y_1) and (x_2, y_2) is $m = \frac{y2 - y1}{x2 - x1}$. For the given points use the values (x_1, y_1) = (-5, 3) and (x_2, y_2)=(-1, -4). Substitute these values into the slope formula and simplify.

$$m = \frac{-4 - 3}{-1 - (-5)}$$
$$m = -\frac{7}{4}$$

27. C: The coordinates of the midpoint of a line with endpoints at (x_1, y_1) and (x_2, y_2) are $(\frac{x_1 + x_2}{2}, \frac{y_1 + y_2}{2})$. For the given endpoints, use the values (x_1, y_1) = (5, 2) and (x_2, y_2)=(-1, 6). Substitute these values into the midpoint formula and simplify.

$$(\frac{5 + (-1)}{2}, \frac{2 + 6}{2}) = (\frac{4}{2}, \frac{8}{2}) = (2,4)$$

28. 10: There are two ways to tackle this problem: (1) The first way is to find coordinates of A using the midpoint formula and then use the distance formula to find the length of AB. (2)

The second way is to find the length of *MB* using the distance formula and then double it since the midpoint is exactly halfway between *A* and B. For the purposes of this explanation, we will use method (2).

First find the distance between *M* and *B* using the distance formula.

$$MB = \sqrt{(x_M - x_B)^2 + (y_M - y_B)^2}$$
$$MB = \sqrt{(3 - 0)^2 + (6 - 2)^2}$$
$$MB = \sqrt{3^2 + 4^2}$$
$$MB = \sqrt{9 + 16}$$
$$MB = \sqrt{25}$$
$$MB = 5$$

Therefore, the length of *MB* is 5. Doubling this number gives the length of *AB*, 5(2) = 10.

29. D: The perimeter of a figure is the length around it. To find the perimeter of a polygon, add the lengths of its sides. Start by filling in the missing lengths of the sides. For instance, the length of the rightmost side is 16 since it must be as long as the leftmost side.

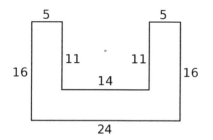

Then add them together to find the perimeter: 5+5+16+11+14+11+16+24=102

30. A: First draw a picture to better visualize the problem. In the diagram to the right, the blue circle represents the fountain and the grey area represents the concrete pathway. To find the area of the pathway, calculate the areas of the larger circle and the smaller circle using the formula for the area of a circle *A=πr²*. Then subtract.

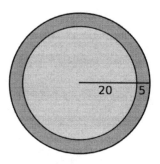

Start with the area of the larger circle. Its radius is 20 + 5 = 25. Use this to calculate its area.

$$A = \pi(25^2)$$
$$A = 625\pi$$
$$A \approx 1963.5$$

Then find the area of the smaller circle.

$$A = \pi(202)$$
$$A = 400\pi$$
$$A \approx 1256.6$$

- 116 -

Finally, subtract the two results to find the area of the concrete pathway and round to the nearest whole number. Since 1963.5 - 1256.6 = 706.9, the area is about 707 square feet.

31. C: A sector is a slice of a sector bounded by two radii. The area of a circle is given by the formula $A=\pi r^2$, where r is the length of the radius. The area of a sector is proportional to the angle between the two radii bounding the sector. The formula for the area of a sector with angle θ given in degrees is $A = \pi r^2 \left(\frac{\theta}{360}\right)$. Substitute the value of the radius and angle into this formula and simplify. Round the result to the nearest tenth.

$$A = \pi r^2 \left(\frac{\theta}{360}\right)$$
$$A = \pi(10^2)\left(\frac{70}{360}\right)$$
$$A \approx 61.1$$

32. D: A sector is a slice of a sector bounded by two radii. In other words, for this problem, you can think of the circle as being divided into 15 equal slices. Therefore, the arc length of each slice is the total arc length of the circle, 360°, divided by 15, which is 24°

33. B: This problem can be solved using the Pythagorean theorem, $a^2 + b^2 = c^2$, twice. To see how this is possible, draw a diagonal n in the front face of the cube.

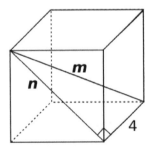

Notice that lines n, m, and a side of the cube form a right triangle inside the cube. We already know the side of the cube is 4, so start by finding the length of line n. To do this, you can either use the Pythagorean theorem or recognize that line n is the hypotenuse of a 45-45-90 right triangle so its length is $\sqrt{2}$ times the length of the legs, or $4\sqrt{2}$. Now find the length of m by using the Pythagorean Theorem.

$$4^2 + \left(4\sqrt{2}\right)^2 = c^2$$
$$16 + 32 = c^2$$
$$48 = c^2$$
$$4\sqrt{3} = c$$

34. A: A cylinder has two congruent circular bases and a lateral edge that, if cut and rolled out, would be a rectangle. Consequently, the formula for the volume of a cylinder with radius r and height h is $A = 2\pi rh + 2\pi r^2$. The problem gives the diameter of the cylinder as 5, so its radius is 5/2 = 2.5. Substitute the values of the radius and height into the formula and calculate.

$$A = 2\pi(2.5)(8) + 2\pi(2.5^2)$$
$$A = 40\pi + 12.5\pi$$
$$A = 52.5\pi$$
$$A \approx 165$$

35. C: The formula for the volume of a pyramid is $V = \frac{1}{3}Bh$, where B is the area of the base and h is the height of the pyramid. The base of a regular square pyramid is a square. Therefore, the area of the base of the Great Pyramid is $750^2 = 562,500$ square feet. To find the pyramid's volume, substitute this value and the height of the pyramid, 450 feet, into the formula and calculate.

$$V = \frac{1}{3}(562,600)(450)$$
$$V = 84,375,000$$

36. C: The probability that the dart hits the marked area is the area of the marked area divided by the area of the whole dartboard. To begin, the area of the whole dartboard can be calculated using the formula $A=\pi r^2$.
$$A = \pi(12^2)$$
$$A = 144\pi$$
The area of the whole dartboard is 144π square in.

The marked area is a sector with a sector missing. Therefore, to find its area, find the area of the larger sector and the smaller missing sector and then subtract. Use the formula for the area of a sector, $A = \pi r^2\left(\frac{\theta}{360}\right)$. Since the dartboard is divided into eight equal sectors, the angle, θ, is $360°/8 = 45°$. Calculate the area of the larger sector, which is a sector of a circle with radius 12 in.
$$A = \pi(12^2)\left(\frac{45}{360}\right)$$
$$A = 144\pi\left(\frac{45}{360}\right)$$
$$A = 18\pi$$

Then find the area of the missing sector. It is from the smaller circle with radius 6 in.
$$A = \pi(6^2)\left(\frac{45}{360}\right)$$
$$A = 36\pi\left(\frac{45}{360}\right)$$
$$A = \frac{9}{2}\pi$$

Now subtract to find the area of the marked region.
$$18\pi - \frac{9}{2}\pi = \frac{27}{2}\pi$$
Thus, the area of the marked region is $\frac{27}{2}\pi$ square in. Divide this by the area of the whole dartboard, 144π square in., to find the probability that the dart hits the marked region.

$$\frac{\frac{27}{2}\pi}{144\pi} = 3/32$$

37. 10: Since there are 12 inches in a foot, we need to find the number of times 3 cm goes into 12 inches. First convert 12 inches into centimeters. There are 2.54 cm in one inch, so the length of the one-foot board is 12(2.54) = 30.48 cm. Now divide 30.48 by 3 to find the number of 3-cm segments that the builder can cut the board into. The result is 30.48/3 = 10.16, so the builder can cut the original board into 10 full segments with a little left over.

38. D: If a pair of parallel lines is cut by a transversal, then corresponding angles are congruent. Angles *1* and *5* are corresponding angles. In addition, vertical angles (angles on the opposite sides of an intersection) are congruent as well. Therefore, angle *8* is congruent to angle *5*. Consequently, angle *1* and *8* are congruent.

39. B: The sum of the measures of the interior angles of a polygon with *n* sides is 180(*n*-2). An octagon has eight sides. Therefore, substitute 8 for *n* into the formula and calculate.

$$180(8 - 2) = 180(6) = 1080$$

40. B: A tangent is a line that intersects a circle at exactly one point (i.e. it just barely touches the circle).A tangent to a given circle is always perpendicular to the circle's radius.

41. A: Notice that line segments *AC* and *BC* are perpendicular. Therefore, the measure of *ABC* is 90° and arc *AB* is 90°. In a circle, the measure of an inscribed angle is equal to one half of the measure of the intercepted arc. Since angle *ADB* is an inscribed angle, its measure is half of the arc length of *AB*, or 90/2 = 45°.

42. D: A translation is a transformation in which a figure slides to another position but retains its size and orientation. In a rotation, a figure turns about some fixed point. In a reflection, a figure flips over a line so that it appears to be backwards (or upside down as the case may be). A transformation is a said to *preserve angle measures* if the angle measures of a figure do not change after the transformation is made. All three of the choices preserve angle measures. Therefore, the answer is D.

43. A: In the figure, you can already see that two pairs of sides are equal (*AB* ≅ *CD* and *BC* ≅ *AD*) since they have the same length. In addition, for both triangles, the remaining side is *AC*. Because a side is always congruent to itself, we can conclude that triangles *ABC* and *ACD* have three congruent sides. As the name suggests, postulate SSS (side-side-side) applies to triangles with three congruent sides. Therefore, we use postulate SSS to conclude that the triangles themselves are also congruent.

44. B: We can show that triangles *ACD* and *BCD* are congruent by SAS (side-angle-side) as follows: (S) We are given that sides *AC* and *BD* are congruent. (A) In addition, because of perpendicular lines, angles *ACD* and *CDB* are right angles and are therefore also congruent. (S) Lastly, the next side for both triangles is *CD*. A side is always congruent to itself.

Since the triangles are congruent, their corresponding angles are also congruent. Angles *A* and *B* are corresponding angles. Therefore, they are congruent.

45. B: The scale factor given in the problem is the ratio of the side lengths of the replica to the side lengths of the original. Since the scale factor is 1:6, divide the dimensions of the original by 6 to find the dimensions of the replica:.

$$\frac{30}{6} = 5$$

$$\frac{21}{6} = 3\frac{1}{2}$$

Thus, the dimension of the replica are 5 in. × $3\frac{1}{2}$ in.

46. C: If two polygons are similar, then the lengths of their corresponding sides are proportional. Write a proportion between the lengths of one pair of corresponding sides and the missing length. Use the variable x for the missing length.

$$\frac{4}{10} = \frac{9}{x}$$

$$4x = 90$$

$$x = \frac{45}{2}$$

47. C: If two polygons are similar, then the lengths of their corresponding sides are proportional. In other words, we can set up a proportion between the lengths of the shortest sides of each rectangle and the lengths of their longest sides. Set up this proportion and then solve for x.

$$\frac{Shortest\ side\ of\ ABED}{Shortest\ side\ of\ ACFD} = \frac{Longest\ side\ of\ ABED}{Longest\ side\ of\ ACFD}$$

$$\frac{AB}{CF} = \frac{BE}{AC}$$

$$\frac{2}{x} = \frac{x}{8}$$

$$16 = x^2$$

$$4 = x$$

48. D: Light striking an object forms a right triangle with the shadow being horizontal, the object vertical, and the light rays as the hypotenuse. Since the light striking the 10-foot pole comes down at the same angle as the light striking the man (remember that it is at the same time of day), the right triangles formed in each case are similar.

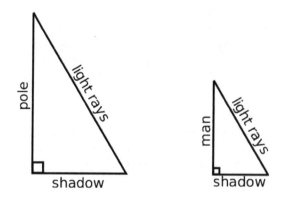

Therefore, use the triangles' similarity to write a proportion and then solve. Use h for the height of the man.

$$\frac{6}{10} = \frac{3.5}{h}$$
$$6h = 35$$
$$h = 5\frac{5}{6}$$

Thus, the man is $5\frac{5}{6}$ feet tall, or 5 ft 10 in.

49. C: Lines AE and AC are transversals of parallel lines BD and CE. As a result, angles ABD and C and angles ADB and E are both sets of corresponding angles. Corresponding angles are congruent. Therefore, triangles ABD and ACE have two angles that are congruent because they are corresponding, and for both the other angle is angle A. Thus, they are similar triangles.

If two polygons are similar, then the lengths of their corresponding sides are proportional. In other words, since BD and CE are corresponding sides, we can set up a proportion between the ratio of their lengths and the ratio of two other corresponding sides.

$$\frac{BD}{CE} = \frac{AB}{AC}$$
$$\frac{4}{x} = \frac{8}{8+4}$$
$$\frac{4}{x} = \frac{8}{12}$$
$$8x = 48$$
$$x = 6$$

50. B: If the altitude is drawn to the hypotenuse of a right triangle, then the two resulting right triangles are similar to each other and to the original right triangle. We are trying to find x, the length of AB. This side is part of both triangle ABD and triangle ABC. Therefore, write a proportion between the corresponding sides of these two triangles and solve for x.

$$\frac{AB}{BC} = \frac{BD}{AB}$$
$$\frac{x}{4} = \frac{4+12}{x}$$
$$\frac{x}{4} = \frac{16}{x}$$
$$x^2 = 64$$
$$x = 8$$

51. 54: If two polygons are similar, then the lengths of their corresponding sides are proportional. The ratio between their corresponding sides is called the similarity ratio. To find this value for the similar quadrilaterals in the problem, divide the lengths of their shortest sides. The shortest sides are 8 and 4. Therefore, the similarity ratio between $ABCD$ and $EFGH$ is 8/4, which simplifies to 2/1.

Since corresponding sides are in the proportion 2 to 1, the perimeters are also in this ratio. Calculate the perimeter of *ABCD* by adding: 4 + 6 + 7 + 10 = 27. The perimeter of *EFGH* is twice the perimeter of *ABCD*, so the answer is 2(27) = 54.

52. C: If the ratio of the corresponding linear dimensions of two similar figures is a/b, then the ratio of their volumes is $(a/b)^3$. In other words, if their lengths (or widths or heights) are multiplied by n, then their volumes are multiplied by n^3. Since the model and actual building are similar and we are given both of their heights, we should start by calculating the ratio of the height of the actual building to the height of model.

The model is 6 inches tall, which is the same as half of a foot. Therefore, the ratio is 20/(1/2), or 40/1. Cube this ratio, and then multiply the result by the volume of the model, which is 4 cubic feet.

$$V = (40/1)^3(4) = 64,000(4) = 256,000$$

Practice Test #2

Practice Questions

1. What is the name of Euclid's most famous work?

Ⓐ Elements

Ⓑ Principia Mathematica

Ⓒ Treatise

Ⓓ On the Equilibrium of Spheres

2. What is the name given to a statement that is not proved but is still considered true because it is thought to be self-evident?

Ⓐ An axiom

Ⓑ A corollary

Ⓒ A definition

Ⓓ A theorem

3. Which statement is true in Euclidean geometry but false in non-Euclidean geometry?

Ⓐ A rectangle is a two-dimensional figure

Ⓑ The sum of the angles of a triangle is always $360°$

Ⓒ The shortest line between two points is a great circle

Ⓓ Parallel lines are a constant distance from one another

4. Write the inverse of the statement "If a man is unmarried, then he is a bachelor".

Ⓐ "If a man is married, then he is not a bachelor"

Ⓑ "If a man is married, then he is a bachelor"

Ⓒ "If a man is not a bachelor, then he is married"

Ⓓ "If a man is a bachelor, then he is unmarried"

5. Which statement is logically equivalent to "If Mary is 15 years old, then she is in the tenth grade"?

Ⓐ "If Mary is not 15 years old, then she is not in the tenth grade"

Ⓑ "If Mary is in the tenth grade, then she is 15 years old"

Ⓒ "If Mary is not in the tenth grade, then she is not 15 years old"

Ⓓ All of the above

6. Which of the following is a counterexample for the statement "If today is the weekend, then it is Sunday"?

Ⓐ It is before 6 pm on Sunday

Ⓑ Today is Saturday

Ⓒ Tomorrow is Saturday

Ⓓ It is Monday morning

7. Find a counterexample for the statement "Every number is either positive or negative".

8. A famous mathematician noted that when n is an integer between 0 and 40, the algebraic expression n^2+n+41 results in a prime number. He therefore conjectured that n^2+n+41 is a prime number for every positive integer n. Which type of reasoning did he use?

Ⓐ Indirect reasoning

Ⓑ Deductive reasoning

Ⓒ Inductive reasoning

Ⓓ Circular reasoning

9. Use inductive reasoning to formulate a conjecture about the sum of the first n powers of two (starting with $n=0$) added to one.

Ⓐ It is a power of two

Ⓑ It is perfect square

Ⓒ It is prime number

Ⓓ It is perfect number

10. Quadrilateral *ABCD* is a parallelogram. Every parallelogram has two pairs of congruent angles. What type of reasoning allows us to therefore conclude that quadrilateral *ABCD* has two pairs of congruent angles?

Ⓐ Deductive reasoning

Ⓑ Indirect reasoning

Ⓒ Inductive reasoning

Ⓓ Circular reasoning

11. A quadrilateral can be divided into two triangles. A pentagon can be divided into three triangles. In general, adding an additional side to a polygon adds another triangle to the division. Use this pattern to write an algebraic expression for the number of triangles a polygon with *n* sides can be divided into.

Ⓐ $\frac{1}{2}n-2$

Ⓑ $\frac{1}{2}n$

Ⓒ $n-2$

Ⓓ n

12. Write an algebraic expression, using the variable _n_, for the number of black dots in the three figures below.

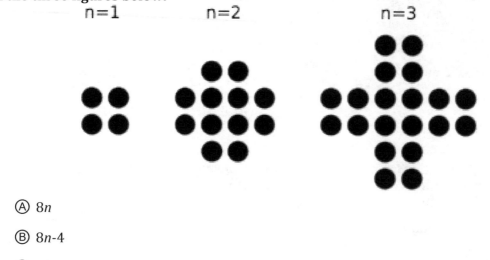

n=1   n=2   n=3

Ⓐ 8n

Ⓑ 8n-4

Ⓒ 10n

Ⓓ 10n-6

13. An isosceles right triangle whose smallest side is 2 feet long has an area of 2 square feet. When the side length is increased to 4 feet, the area becomes 8 square feet. And when it is 8 feet, the area is 32 square feet. Make a generalization about the relationship between the side length of an isosceles right triangle and its area.

Ⓐ The area of an isosceles right triangle is always 1 or 2 times the side length.

Ⓑ The ratio of the side length and the area is in the proportion 1:2

Ⓒ When the side length doubles, the area quadruples

Ⓓ When the side length increases by 2, the area increases by 6

14. What transformation is represented by the figure below?

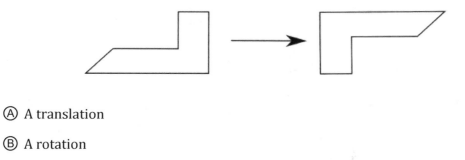

Ⓐ A translation

Ⓑ A rotation

Ⓒ A dilation

Ⓓ A reflection

15. Which triangle is a right triangle?

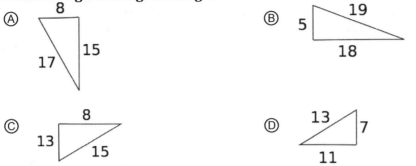

16. In a right triangle, the length of one leg is 12/13 of the length of the hypotenuse. What fraction of the length of the hypotenuse is the length of the other leg?

Ⓐ 1/12

Ⓑ 5/12

Ⓒ 1/13

Ⓓ 5/13

17. In a 30-60-90 triangle, the lengths of two sides are $3\sqrt{3}$ and 6. What is the length of the third side?

Ⓐ 3

Ⓑ 6

Ⓒ $3\sqrt{2}$

Ⓓ $3\sqrt{3}$

18. To make wooden triangular supports for a wall, 3 in. by 3 in. squares are cut in half by cutting from one corner to the opposite corner. What is length of the hypotenuse of the resulting triangular support in inches? Round to the nearest inch.

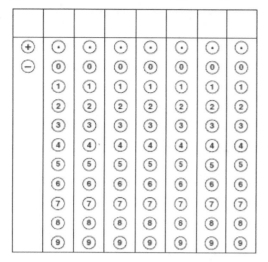

19. Which of the following is a net of a square pyramid?

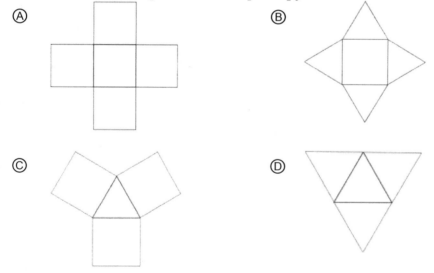

Ⓐ

Ⓑ

Ⓒ

Ⓓ

20. If two distinct planes intersect, what shape is their intersection?

Ⓐ A plane

Ⓑ A line

Ⓒ A triangle

Ⓓ A rectangle

21. Which graph represents the triangle with vertices at (-1,2), (5,8), and (7,4)?

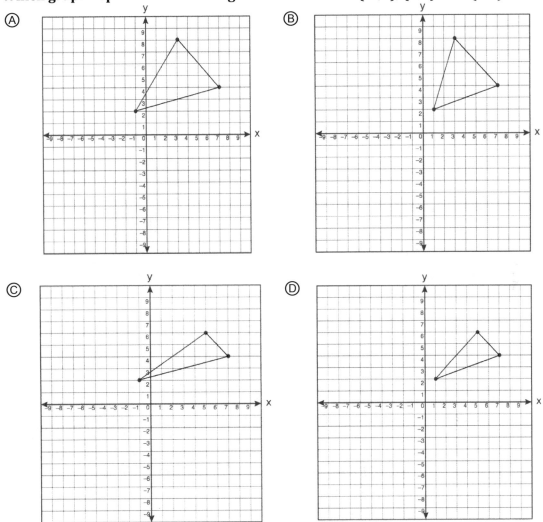

22. What kinds of lines have slopes equal to zero?

Ⓐ Parallel lines

Ⓑ Vertical lines

Ⓒ Horizontal lines

Ⓓ None of the above

23. Which line appears to have a slope of -2?

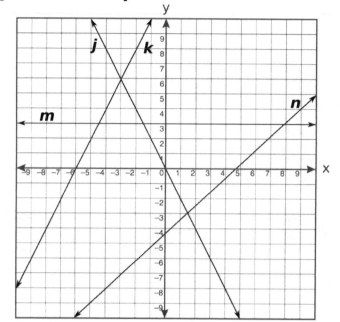

Ⓐ Line *j*

Ⓑ Line *k*

Ⓒ Line *m*

Ⓓ Line *n*

24. The slope of a line, *AB*, containing A (4, -3) and B (7, *k*) is 2. What is the value of *k*?

Ⓐ -9

Ⓑ -7/2

Ⓒ -3/2

Ⓓ 3

25. The equation of line *L* is $y = 3x - 5$ Find an equation of the line that is perpendicular to L and intersects it at (3, 4).

Ⓐ $y = -\frac{1}{3}x + 2$

Ⓑ $y = -x + 5$

Ⓒ $y = \frac{1}{3}x + 2$

Ⓓ $y = \frac{1}{3}x + 5$

26. What is the slope of the line that contains _A_ (-5, 3) and _B_ (-1, -4)?

Ⓐ -1/4

Ⓑ -7/4

Ⓒ -1/6

Ⓓ 7/6

27. What is the midpoint of the line segment with endpoints at _A_ (7, 1) and _B_ (-3, 3)?

Ⓐ (2, 2)

Ⓑ (3, 2)

Ⓒ (5, -1)

Ⓓ (5, 1)

28. The midpoint between two points, _A_ and _B_, is _M_ (-1, 5). If the coordinates of B are (4,-7), what is length of line _AB_?

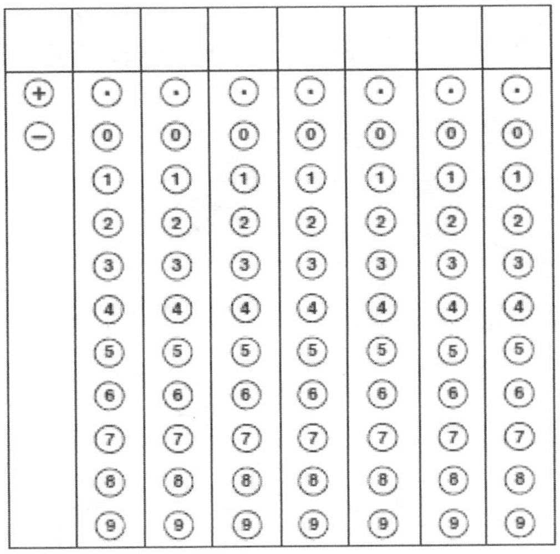

⊕	•	•	•	•	•	•	•
⊖	⓪	⓪	⓪	⓪	⓪	⓪	⓪
	①	①	①	①	①	①	①
	②	②	②	②	②	②	②
	③	③	③	③	③	③	③
	④	④	④	④	④	④	④
	⑤	⑤	⑤	⑤	⑤	⑤	⑤
	⑥	⑥	⑥	⑥	⑥	⑥	⑥
	⑦	⑦	⑦	⑦	⑦	⑦	⑦
	⑧	⑧	⑧	⑧	⑧	⑧	⑧
	⑨	⑨	⑨	⑨	⑨	⑨	⑨

29. In the figure, all angles are right angles. Calculate the perimeter of the figure.

Ⓐ 36

Ⓑ 48

Ⓒ 60

Ⓓ 64

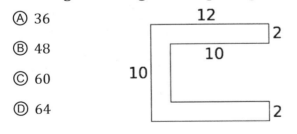

30. An architect plans to build a circular pathway around a fountain that has a radius of 25 feet. The pathway will be made of concrete and be 5 feet wide. What will be the area of the pathway when it is complete? Round your answer to the nearest square foot.

(A) 864 square feet

(B) 1256 square feet.

(C) 1963 square feet

(D) 2827 square feet

31. The radius of the circle to the right is 12. Find the area of the shaded sector. Round to the nearest tenth.

(A) 5.2

(B) 20.0

(C) 62.8

(D) 452.4

32. A circle is divided into 20 congruent sectors. What is the arc length of each sector?

(A) 2°

(B) 9°

(C) 15°

(D) 18°

33. The cube in the figure to the right has sides of length 6. Find the length of line *m*, which travels from one corner of a cube to the opposite corner.

(A) $6\sqrt{2}$

(B) $6\sqrt{3}$

(C) 12

(D) $12\sqrt{2}$

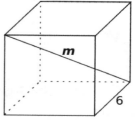

34. What is the surface area of a cone with a diameter of 3 and a slant height of 4? Round to the nearest whole number.

Ⓐ 26

Ⓑ 45

Ⓒ 66

Ⓓ 104

35. The Red Pyramid in Dahshur, Egypt is a regular square pyramid roughly 340 feet tall and 720 feet long on each side. Assuming it is a regular square pyramid, what is its volume?

Ⓐ 81,600 cubic feet

Ⓑ 27,744,000 cubic feet

Ⓒ 58,752,000 cubic feet

Ⓓ 176,256,000 cubic feet

36. In the dartboard to the right, the radius of the smaller circle is 3 in. and the radius of the larger one is 6 in. If a dart is thrown at the dartboard, what is the probability that it hits somewhere in the section marked by the X?

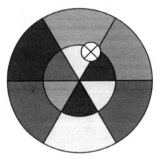

Ⓐ 1/24

Ⓑ 1/8

Ⓒ 1/6

Ⓓ 1/4

37. A builder wants to cut a two-foot board into segments that are 4 cm long. How many full segments can he cut?

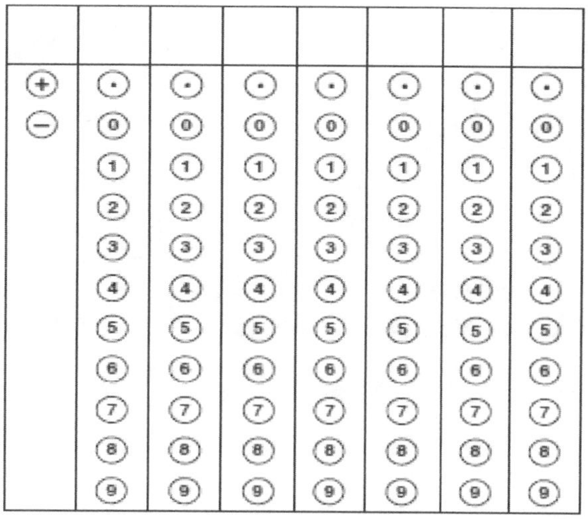

⊕	·	·	·	·	·	·	·
⊖	0	0	0	0	0	0	0
	1	1	1	1	1	1	1
	2	2	2	2	2	2	2
	3	3	3	3	3	3	3
	4	4	4	4	4	4	4
	5	5	5	5	5	5	5
	6	6	6	6	6	6	6
	7	7	7	7	7	7	7
	8	8	8	8	8	8	8
	9	9	9	9	9	9	9

38. In the figure to the right, line m is parallel to line n. Which angle must be congruent to angle 3?

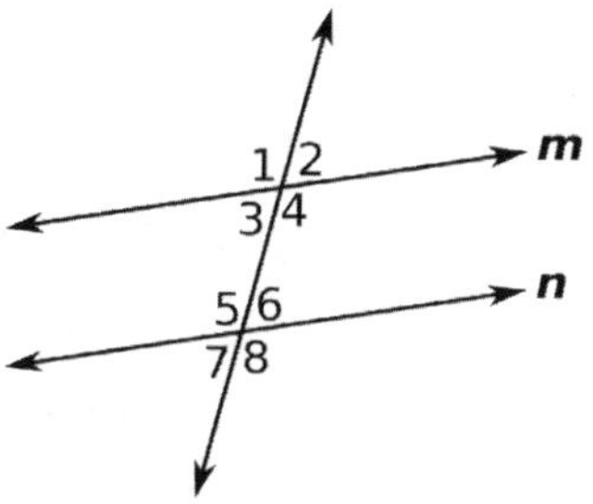

Ⓐ Angle *4*

Ⓑ Angle *5*

Ⓒ Angle *6*

Ⓓ Angle *8*

39. What is the sum of the measures of the interior angles of a hexagon?

Ⓐ 540°

Ⓑ 720°

Ⓒ 960°

Ⓓ 1080°

40. If a line is tangent to a circle, at how many points does it intersect the circle?

Ⓐ 0

Ⓑ 1

Ⓒ 2

Ⓓ 3

41. In the figure to the right, C is the center of the circle. Calculate the value of x.

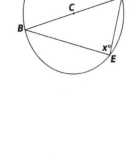

Ⓐ 45

Ⓑ 67.5

Ⓒ 90

Ⓓ 95

42. Which of the following transformations preserves distance?

Ⓐ Translation

Ⓑ Rotation

Ⓒ Reflection

Ⓓ All of the above

43. In the figure to the right, which postulate most directly allows us to conclude that triangle ABC is congruent to ACD?

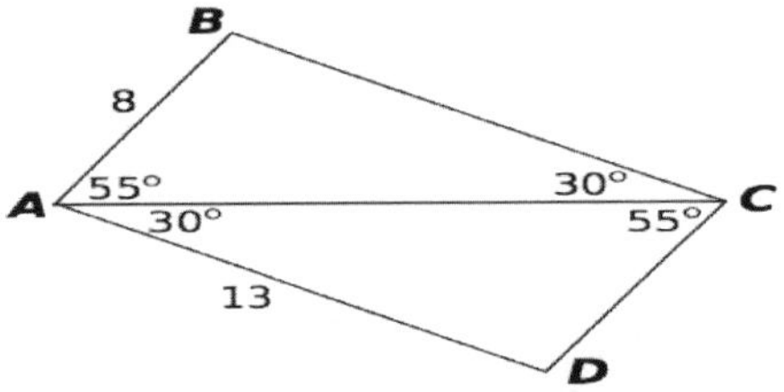

Ⓐ Postulate SSS

Ⓑ Postulate SAS

Ⓒ Postulate ASA

Ⓓ Postulate AAS

44. In the figure to the right, AB is parallel to DE. Which of the following must also be true?

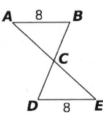

Ⓐ AC is congruent to CE

Ⓑ Angle A is congruent to angle B

Ⓒ Triangles ABC and CDE are isosceles triangles

Ⓓ Angle B is a right angle

45. An artist makes a replica of Picasso's *Guernica* for a postcard. To make the replica, he uses 1 inch on the postcard to represent 12 inches in the original. If the original painting is about 138 in. × 306 in., what are the dimensions of the replica?

Ⓐ 1 in. × 2 in.

Ⓑ $11\frac{1}{2}$ in. × $25\frac{1}{2}$ in.

Ⓒ 13 in. × $30\frac{1}{2}$ in.

Ⓓ 23 in. × 51 in.

46. The lengths of the sides of triangle *ABC* are 2, 6, and 7. The lengths of the shortest two sides of similar triangle *DEF* are 5 and 15. What is the length of the longest side of *DEF*?

Ⓐ 21/4

Ⓑ 21/2

Ⓒ 35/2

Ⓓ 35

47. In the figure below, the shaded rectangle *ABED* is similar to the large rectangle *ACDF*. What is the value of *x*?

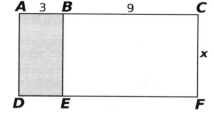

Ⓐ 5/2

Ⓑ 3

Ⓒ 4

Ⓓ 6

48. At a certain time of day, a 12-foot pole casts a 5-foot shadow. How tall is a man who casts a $2\frac{1}{2}$ foot shadow at the same time of day?

Ⓐ 5 ft

Ⓑ 5 ft 3 in

Ⓒ 5 ft 8 in

Ⓓ 6 ft

49. In the figure to the right, *BD* is parallel to *CE*. Use similar triangles to find the length of *CE*.

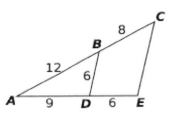

Ⓐ 4

Ⓑ 6

Ⓒ 10

Ⓓ 12

50. The figure to the right contains a right triangle *ABD* with its altitude drawn. Use the similarity properties of right triangles to find the value of *x*.

Ⓐ 3

Ⓑ 6

Ⓒ 8

Ⓓ 9

51. The lengths of the sides of a pentagon *ABCDE* are 2, 3, 5, 8, and 10. What is the perimeter of similar pentagon *FGHIJ* if the length of its shortest side is 4?

⊕	·	·	·	·	·	·	·
⊖	0	0	0	0	0	0	0
	1	1	1	1	1	1	1
	2	2	2	2	2	2	2
	3	3	3	3	3	3	3
	4	4	4	4	4	4	4
	5	5	5	5	5	5	5
	6	6	6	6	6	6	6
	7	7	7	7	7	7	7
	8	8	8	8	8	8	8
	9	9	9	9	9	9	9

52. To help plan a building, an architect makes a model of it that is 6 inches tall with a total volume of 5 cubic feet. Calculate the volume of the actual building if it will be 30 feet tall.

Ⓐ 300 ft³

Ⓑ $\frac{8000}{27}$ ft³

Ⓒ 1,080,000 ft³

Ⓓ 2,160,000 ft³

Answers and Explanations

1. A: Euclid, a Greek mathematician who lived around 300 BC, is usually considered the father of geometry and an important figure in the development of the notion of mathematical rigor. His most famous work is *Elements*, a collection of geometric proofs, starting with definitions and axioms and proceeding to more complicated propositions. It was still a widely read work until the 20th century.

2. A: Every branch of mathematics, including geometry, begins with basic definitions and unproven statements, called either axioms or postulates. New propositions, called theorems, are proved using deductive logic and previously established statements. Theorems that easily follow from another theorem are called corollaries.

3. D: Non-Euclidean geometry is geometry in which the parallel postulate is assumed to be false. Pictorially, this means that Euclidean geometry is on a flat plane (it is the geometry we are most familiar with), whereas non-Euclidean geometry is on a curved surface. As a result, parallel lines are a constant distance from one another in Euclidean geometry. On the other hand, in non-Euclidean geometry, parallel lines either curve away or toward one another depending on whether the surface is curved like a saddle-shaped plane or an ellipsoid.

4. A: The inverse of a statement "If p, then q" is "If $\sim p$, then $\sim q$", where p and q are any statement and the tilde ($\sim$) means "not" or "the opposite of". In other words, to construct the converse, negate (find the opposite of) both halves of the original statement. In the given expression, the p-statement is "a man is unmarried" and the q-statement is "he [a man] is a bachelor". Since being *not unmarried* is the same as being *married*, the inverse is "If a man married, then he is not a bachelor".

5. C: A conditional and its contrapositive always have the same truth table, so they are considered logically equivalent. On the other hand, the inverse and converse do not have the same truth table as the original statement, so they are not considered logically equivalent. Examine the choices A, B, and C and notice that choice A is the inverse of the original statement, choice B is the converse, and choice C is the contrapositive. Therefore, only the statement in choice C is logically equivalent to the original statement.

6. B: A counterexample is a specific example that violates a general statement. Since the given statement "If today is the weekend, then it is Sunday" is a conditional (i.e. it is in the form "If..., then..."), a counterexample will be an example in which the "if" part of the statement is true, but the "then" part is false. Therefore, for this problem, we need to find a day that is part of the weekend but is not Sunday. The only day that fits that description is Saturday.

7. 0: A counterexample is a specific example that violates a general statement. Since the statement is "Every number is either positive or negative", a counterexample would be a number that is neither positive nor negative. The only number that is neither positive nor negative is 0.

8. C: Inductive reasoning involves making an observation, finding a pattern, and making a general conjecture based on that pattern. In this example, the pattern the mathematician found was that, when n is an integer between 0 and 40, n^2+n+41 is a prime number. Using inductive reasoning, he generalized this pattern of 41 values of *n* to apply to all integer values of *n*.

9. A: Inductive reasoning involves making an observation, finding a pattern, and making a general conjecture based on that pattern. When *n* is between 0 and 4, the sum of the first *n* powers of two added to one are:

$$(2^0) + 1 = 1 + 1 = 2$$
$$(2^0 + 2^1) + 1 = (1 + 2) + 1 = 4$$
$$(2^0 + 2^1 + 2^2) + 1 = (1 + 2 + 4) + 1 = 8$$
$$(2^0 + 2^1 + 2^2 + 2^3) + 1 = (1 + 2 + 4 + 8) + 1 = 16$$

Notice that these numbers are all powers of two. Therefore, using inductive reasoning, we can make the conjecture the sum of the first *n* powers of two added to one is itself a power of two. Although this type of reasoning is not considered a valid method of mathematical proof, it is still useful for discovering possible theorems that can later be proved rigorously.

10. A: Deductive reasoning asserts conclusion that must necessarily be true based on a set of premises. In this problem, the premises are "Quadrilateral *ABCD* is a parallelogram" and "Every parallelogram has two pairs of congruent angles". Since quadrilateral *ABCD* is an instance of a parallelogram, it must *necessarily* have two pairs of congruent angles. Therefore, this is an example of deductive reasoning.

11. C: From the problem, a quadrilateral can be divided into two triangles. So, when *n* = 4, the correct algebraic expression will be 2. Plugging in 4 for *n* into the choices eliminates choices A and D right away since they don't result in 2. In addition, the expression should increase by one when *n* increases by one. This tells us that *n* should not have a coefficient in the algebraic expression. Therefore, the answer must be C. Choice B is incorrect because when *n* increases by one, the expression increases by 1/2, not 1.

12. B: Examine the three figures. To organize the information, make a table.

n	# of Dots
1	4
2	12
3	20

Examine the data to find a pattern. Notice that when *n* increases by one, the number of black dots increases by eight. This suggests that the coefficient of *n* should be eight in the algebraic expression. Another important observation is that when *n*=1, there are four dots. As a result, leaving the expression as simply 8*n* will not work because 8(1) = 8. Therefore, you need to offset this difference by subtracting four from 8*n* to get 8*n*-4. To check the expression, substitute 1, 2, and 3, for *n* and calculate the result.

13. C: To organize the information, make a table.

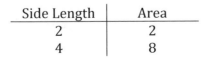

Side Length	Area
2	2
4	8

Examine the data to find a pattern. In the side length column, the numbers are doubled from 2 to 4 and then from 4 to 8. In the area column, the numbers quadruple: 8 is four times 2 and 32 is four times that. Therefore, the pattern is that when the side length of the equilateral triangle double, the area quadruples.

14. B: A translation is a transformation in which a figure slides to another position but retains its size and orientation. In a rotation, a figure turns about some fixed point. In a dilation, a figure changes its size but retains its position and orientation. In a reflection, a figure flips over a line so that it appears to be backwards (or upside down as the case may be). Notice that in the figure above, the figure appears to be rotated 180°.

15. A: If a triangle is a right triangle, then the lengths of its sides obey the Pythagorean theorem, $a^2 + b^2 = c^2$. To determine which triangle is right, test each triangle by substituting its side lengths into the Pythagorean theorem. Start with the first triangle.

$$8^2 + 15^2 =? 17^2$$
$$64 + 225 =? 289$$
$$289 = 289$$

The first triangle obeys the Pythagorean theorem. Therefore, it is a right triangle. You can check the other three triangles to see that they do not work.

16. D: In this problem, the exact lengths of the sides are neither given nor asked for. Instead, we are dealing with a right triangle in which the proportion of the lengths is fixed. To make the problem easier to work with, it is okay to give the sides of the triangle specific number lengths. Let's use 13 for the length of the hypotenuse.

The length of the leg is 12/13 times the length of the hypotenuse, so it 12. Since this is a right triangle, we can use the Pythagorean theorem to find the missing side or recognize that these numbers are two parts of the Pythagorean triple 5-12-13. Therefore, the missing side is 5. Reread the question again. It asks for a fraction for the length of the leg (5) to the length of the hypotenuse (13). Thus, the answer is 5/13.

17. A: In a 30-60-90 triangle, the ratio of the lengths of the sides are $1: \sqrt{3}: 2$. In other words, the length of the longer leg is $\sqrt{3}$ times the length of the shorter leg, and the hypotenuse is twice the length of the shorter leg. We are already given that two sides are $3\sqrt{3}$ and 6. It may be helpful to draw a triangle as a guide. Since the given lengths are in the ratio $\sqrt{3}: 2$, they must be the longer leg and the hypotenuse. Therefore, the missing side is the shorter leg. To find its length,
divide the length of the hypotenuse, 6, by 2 to get the answer. The answer is 3.

18. 7: The original pieces of wood are squares with 3 in. sides. Therefore, when the squares are cut in half, the resulting triangle is a 45-45-90 triangle. In 45-45-90 triangle, the ratio of the sides is $1: 1: \sqrt{2}$. From the way the squares are cut, we also know that the legs of the triangles are 3 in. long. Thus, to find the length of the hypotenuse, multiply the length of the leg, 3 in., by $\sqrt{2}$ and round to the nearest whole number. The result is 4 in.

19. B: A net is a two-dimensional figure that can be folded into a three-dimensional solid. A square pyramid is a pyramid with a square base. Therefore, it has one square face and four triangular faces. Only choice B has this combination of faces. Thus, it is the answer. Also, notice that you can fold the

20. B: The intersection of two figures in three-dimensional space is the set of points where the two figures meet. If a plane intersects another plane, the intersection is a line as shown in the figure below.

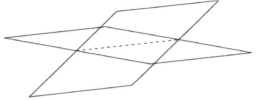

21. C: To graph points on a coordinate axis, start at the origin, (0,0), and move left or right based on the first coordinate (the *x*-coordinate) and then up or down based on the second coordinate (the *y*-coordinate. For instance, to graph the first point, (-1,2), start at the origin and move left one unit and up two units, and then put a dot where you end up. After graphing the three points, (-1,2), (5,8), and (7,4), the result is the triangle in the graph in choice C.

22. C: The formula for the slope *m* of a line containing the points (x_1, y_1) and (x_2, y_2) is $m = \frac{y_2 - y_1}{x_2 - x_1}$. In this formula, the only way the slope can be zero is if the numerator is zero. The numerator will only be zero when $y_2 = y_1$, or, in other words, when the *y*-coordinates of the two points are equal. Two points have the same *y*-coordinates only when they are on the same horizontal line. Therefore, only horizontal lines have slopes equal to zero.

23. A: The slope of a line is a number that represents its steepness. Lines with positive slope go from the bottom-left to the top-right, lines with negative slope go from the top-left to the bottom-right, and horizontal lines have zero slope. You can also think of slope as being $\frac{rise}{run}$. In particular, a slope of -2 (which is equivalent to a slope of -2/1) means that the line falls (goes down) 2 units every time it runs (goes to the right) 1 unit. Looking closely at line *j*, notice that for every 2 units it goes down, it goes to the right 1 unit.

24. D: The formula for the slope *m* of a line containing the points (x_1, y_1) and (x_2, y_2) is $m = \frac{y_2 - y_1}{x_2 - x_1}$. Substitute the coordinates of the given points, *A* and *B*, into the formula and set the slope *m* equal to 2. Then solve for *k*.

$$2 = \frac{k - (-3)}{7 - 4}$$
$$2 = \frac{k + 3}{3}$$
$$6 = k + 3$$
$$3 = k$$

Therefore, the value of *k* is 3.

25. B: The given equation of *L* is in slope-intercept form $y = mx + b$, where *m* is the slope of the line and *b* is the *x*-intercept. Consequently, we know that the slope of *L* is 3 and its *x*-

intercept is -5. In addition, every line that is perpendicular to L will have a slope that is the *negative reciprocal* of the slope of L. Since the reciprocal of the slope of L (which is 3) is 1/3, the negative reciprocal is -1/3. So, we now know that the equation for the line perpendicular to L is $y = -\frac{1}{3}x + b$.

To find the y-intercept b, substitute the point (3,4) into the equation and solve for b.

$$4 = -\frac{1}{3}(3) + b$$
$$4 = -1 + b$$
$$5 = b$$

Finally, plug the value of b into the equation. The result is $y = -\frac{1}{3}x + 5$.

26. B: The formula for the slope m of a line containing the points (x_1, y_1) and (x_2, y_2) is $m = \frac{y_2 - y_1}{x_2 - x_1}$. For the given points use the values (x_1, y_1) = (-5, 3) and (x_2, y_2) = (-1, -4). Substitute these values into the slope formula and simplify.

$$m = \frac{-4 - 3}{-1 - (-5)}$$
$$m = -7/4$$

27. A: The coordinates of the midpoint of a line with endpoints at (x_1, y_1) and (x_2, y_2) are $(\frac{x1+x2}{2}, \frac{y1+y2}{2})$. For the given endpoints, use the values (x_1, y_1) = (7, 1) and (x_2, y_2)=(-3, 3). Substitute these values into the midpoint formula and simplify.

$$(\frac{7 + (-3)}{2}, \frac{1 + 3}{2}) = (\frac{4}{2}, \frac{4}{2}) = (2,2)$$

28. 26: There are two ways to tackle this problem: (1) The first way is to find coordinates of A using the midpoint formula and then use the distance formula to find the length of AB. (2) The second way is to find the length of MB using the distance formula and then double it since the midpoint is exactly halfway between A and B. For the purposes of this explanation, we will use method (2).

First find the distance between M and B using the distance formula.
$$MB = \sqrt{(x_M - x_B)^2 + (y_M - y_B)^2}$$
$$MB = \sqrt{(-1 - 4)^2 + (5 - (-7))^2}$$
$$MB = \sqrt{(-5)^2 + 12^2}$$
$$MB = \sqrt{25 + 144}$$
$$MB = \sqrt{169}$$
$$MB = 13$$

Therefore, the length of MB is 13. Doubling this number gives the length of AB, 2(13) = 26.

29. D: The perimeter of a figure is the length around it. To find the perimeter of a polygon, add the lengths of its sides. Start by filling in the missing lengths of the sides. For instance, the length of the bottommost side is 12 since it must be as long as the topmost side.

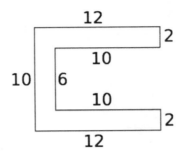

Then add them together to find the perimeter: 12 + 2 + 10 + 10 + 6 + 10 + 2 + 12 = 64.

30. A: First draw a picture to better visualize the problem. In the diagram to the right, the blue circle represents the fountain and the grey area represents the concrete pathway. To find the area of the pathway, calculate the areas of the larger circle and the smaller circle using the formula for the area of a circle A=πr². Then subtract.

Start with the area of the larger circle. Its radius is 25 + 5 = 30. Use this to calculate its area.
$A = \pi(30^2)$
$A = 900\pi$
$A \approx 2827.4$

Then find the area of the smaller circle.
$A = \pi(25^2)$
$A = 625\pi$
$A \approx 1963.5$

Finally, subtract the two results to find the area of the concrete pathway and round to the nearest whole number. Since 2827.4 – 1963.5 = 863.9, the area is about 864 square feet.

31. C: A sector is a slice of a sector bounded by two radii. The area of a circle is given by the formula A = πr², where r is the length of the radius. The area of a sector is proportional to the angle between the two radii bounding the sector. The formula for the area of a sector with angle θ given in degrees is $A = \pi r^2(\frac{\theta}{360})$. Substitute the value of the radius and angle into this formula and simplify. Round the result to the nearest tenth.

$$A = \pi r^2(\frac{\theta}{360})$$
$$A = \pi(12^2)(\frac{50}{360})$$
$$A \approx 62.8$$

32. D: A sector is a slice of a sector bounded by two radii. In other words, for this problem, you can think of the circle as being divided into 20 equal slices. Therefore, the arc length of each slice is the total arc length of the circle, 360°, divided by 20, which is 18°

33. B: This problem can be solved using the Pythagorean theorem, a² + b² = c², twice. To see how this is possible, draw a diagonal *n* in the front face of the cube.

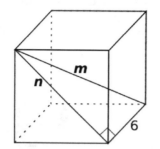

Notice that lines *n*, *m*, and a side of the cube form a right triangle inside the cube. We already know the side of the cube is 6, so start by finding the length of line *n*. To do this, you can either use the Pythagorean theorem or recognize that line *n* is the hypotenuse of a 45-45-90 right triangle so its length is $\sqrt{2}$ times the length of the legs, or $6\sqrt{2}$. Now find the length of *m* by using the Pythagorean theorem.

$$6^2 + \left(6\sqrt{2}\right)^2 = c^2$$
$$36 + 72 = c^2$$
$$108 = c^2$$
$$6\sqrt{3} = c$$

34. A: A cone has a circular base and a lateral edge. The formula for the volume of a cylinder with radius *r* and slant height *l* is $A = \pi r l + \pi r^2$. The problem gives the diameter of the cone as 3, so its radius is 3/2 = 1.5. Substitute the values of the radius and slant height into the formula and calculate.

$$A = \pi(1.5)(4) + \pi(1.5^2)$$
$$A = 6\pi + 2.25\pi$$
$$A = 8.25\pi$$
$$A \approx 26$$

35. C: The formula for the volume of a pyramid is $V = (1/3)Bh$, where *B* is the area of the base and *h* is the height of the pyramid. The base of a regular square pyramid is a square. Therefore, the area of the base of the Great Pyramid is 720² =518,400 square feet. To find the pyramid's volume, substitute this value and the height of the pyramid, 340 feet, into the formula and calculate.
$V = (1/3)(518,400)(340)$
$V = 58,752,000$

36. B: The probability that the dart hits the marked area is the area of the marked area divided by the area of the whole dartboard. To begin, the area of the whole dartboard can be calculated using the formula A=πr².
$$A = \pi(6^2)$$
$$A = 36\pi$$
The area of the whole dartboard is 36π square in.

The marked area is a sector with a sector missing. Therefore, to find its area, find the area of the larger sector and the smaller missing sector and then subtract. Use the formula for the area of a sector, $A = \pi r^2(\theta/360)$. Since the dartboard is divided into six equal sectors, the

- 144 -

angle, θ, is 360°/6=60°. Calculate the area of the larger sector, which is a sector of a circle with radius 6 in.

$$A = \pi(6^2)(60/360)$$
$$A = 36\pi(60/360)$$
$$A = 6\pi$$

Then find the area of the missing sector. It is from the smaller circle with radius 3 in.

$$A = \pi(3^2)(60/360)$$
$$A = 9\pi\left(\frac{60}{360}\right)$$
$$A = \frac{3}{2}\pi$$

Now subtract to find the area of the marked region.

$$A = 6\pi - 3/2\pi = 9/2\pi$$

Thus, the area of the marked region is $\frac{9}{2}\pi$ square in. Divide this by the area of the whole dartboard, 36π square in., to find the probability that the dart hits the marked region.

$$\frac{\frac{9}{2}\pi}{36\pi} = \frac{1}{8}$$

37. 15: Since there are 12 inches in a foot, we need to find the number of times 3 cm goes into 24 inches. First convert 24 inches into centimeters. There are 2.54 cm in one inch, so the length of the one-foot board is 24(2.54) = 60.96 cm. Now divide 60.96 by 4 to find the number of 4-cm segments that the builder can cut the board into. The result is 60.96/4 = 15.24, so the builder can cut the original board into 15 full segments with a little left over.

38. C: If a pair of parallel lines is cut by a transversal, then corresponding angles are congruent. Angles *3* and *7* are corresponding angles. In addition, vertical angles (angles on the opposite sides of an intersection) are congruent as well. Therefore, angle *7* is congruent to angle *6*. Consequently, angle *3* and *6* are congruent.

39. B: The sum of the measures of the interior angles of a polygon with *n* sides is 180(*n*-2). A hexagon has eight sides. Therefore, substitute 6 for *n* into the formula and calculate.

Sum = 180(6 – 2) = 180(4) = 720

40. B: A tangent is a line that intersects a circle at exactly one point (i.e. it just barely touches the circle).

41. C: Notice that line segment *BD* is a straight line. Therefore, the measure of *BCD* is 180° and arc *BAD* is 180°. In a circle, the measure of an inscribed angle is equal to one half of the measure of the intercepted arc. Since angle *BDE* is an inscribed angle, its measure is half of the arc length of *BAD*, or 180/2=90.

42. D: A translation is a transformation in which a figure slides to another position but retains its size and orientation. In a rotation, a figure turns about some fixed point. In a reflection, a figure flips over a line so that it appears to be backwards (or upside down as the case may be). A transformation is a said to *preserve distance* if the lengths of lines in a figure do not change after the transformation is made. All three of the choices preserve distance. Therefore, the answer is D.

43. C: In the figure, you can already see that two pairs of angles are congruent ($BAC \cong ACD$ and $BCA \cong CAD$) since they have the same angle measure. In addition, the triangles share a side, AC, which is between the pairs of congruent angles. Because a side is always congruent to itself, we can therefore conclude that triangles ABC and ACD have two congruent angles and a congruent side between them. As the name suggests, postulate ASA (angle-side-angle) applies to triangles in this situation. Therefore, postulate ASA allows us to conclude that the triangles are congruent.

44. A: We can show that triangles ABC and CDE are congruent by ASA (angle-side-angle) as follows: (A) AB and DE are parallel, and angles A and E are alternating interior angles of the transversal AE, so they are congruent. (S) Lines AB and DE are both have length 8, so they are also congruent. (A) Lastly, Angles B and D are also alternating interior angles, so they are congruent.

Since the triangles are congruent, their corresponding sides are also congruent. AC and CE are corresponding sides. Therefore, they are congruent.

45. B: The scale factor given in the problem is the ratio of the side lengths of the replica to the side lengths of the original. Since the scale factor is 1:12, divide the dimensions of the original by 12 to find the dimensions of the replica:

$$\frac{138}{12} = 11\frac{1}{2}$$
$$\frac{306}{6} = 25\frac{1}{2}$$

Thus, the dimensions of the replica are 11 1/2 in. × 25 1/2 in.

46. C: If two polygons are similar, then the lengths of their corresponding sides are proportional. Write a proportion between the lengths of one pair of corresponding sides and the missing length. Use the variable x for the missing length.

$$\frac{2}{5} = \frac{7}{x}$$
$$2x = 35$$
$$x = \frac{35}{2}$$

47. D: If two polygons are similar, then the lengths of their corresponding sides are proportional. In other words, we can set up a proportion between the lengths of the shortest sides of each rectangle and the lengths of their longest sides. Set up this proportion and then solve for x.

$$\frac{Shortest\ side\ of\ ABED}{Shortest\ side\ of\ ACFD} = \frac{Longest\ side\ of\ ABED}{Longest\ side\ of\ ACFD}$$
$$\frac{AB}{CF} = \frac{BE}{AC}$$
$$\frac{3}{x} = \frac{x}{12}$$
$$36 = x^2$$

- 146 -

$$6 = x$$

48. D: Light striking an object forms a right triangle with the shadow being horizontal, the object vertical, and the light rays as the hypotenuse. Since the light striking the 12-foot pole comes down at the same angle as the light striking the man (remember that it is at the same time of day), the right triangles formed in each case are similar.

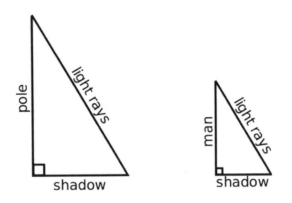

Therefore, use the triangles' similarity to write a proportion and then solve. Use h for the height of the man.

$$\frac{5}{12} = \frac{2.5}{h}$$
$$5h = 30$$
$$h = 6$$

Thus, the man is 6 ft.

49. C: Lines AE and AC are transversals of parallel lines BD and CE. As a result, angles ABD and C and angles ADB and E are both sets of corresponding angles. Corresponding angles are congruent. Therefore, triangles ABD and ACE have two angles that are congruent because they are corresponding, and for both the other angle is angle A. Thus, they are similar triangles.

If two polygons are similar, then the lengths of their corresponding sides are proportional. In other words, since BD and CE are corresponding sides, we can set up a proportion between the ratio of their lengths and the ratio of two other corresponding sides.

$$\frac{BD}{CE} = \frac{AB}{AC}$$
$$\frac{6}{x} = \frac{12}{12 + 8}$$
$$\frac{6}{x} = \frac{12}{20}$$
$$12x = 120$$
$$x = 10$$

50. B: If the altitude is drawn to the hypotenuse of a right triangle, then the two resulting right triangles are similar to each other and to the original right triangle. We are trying to find x, the length of AB. This side is part of both triangle ABD and triangle ABC. Therefore, write a proportion between the corresponding sides of these two triangles and solve for x.

$$\frac{AB}{BC} = \frac{BD}{AB}$$

$$\frac{x}{3} = \frac{3+9}{x}$$

$$\frac{x}{3} = \frac{12}{x}$$

$$x^2 = 36$$

$$x = 6$$

51. 56: If two polygons are similar, then the lengths of their corresponding sides are proportional. The ratio between their corresponding sides is called the similarity ratio. To find this value for the similar quadrilaterals in the problem, divide the lengths of their shortest sides. The shortest sides are 4 and 2. Therefore, the similarity ratio between *ABCDE* and *FGHIJ* is 4/2, which simplifies to 2/1.

Since corresponding sides are in the proportion 2 to 1, the perimeters are also in this ratio. Calculate the perimeter of *ABCDE* by adding: 2 + 3 + 5 + 8 + 10 = 28. The perimeter of *FGHIJ* is twice the perimeter of *ABCDE*, so the answer is 2(28)=56.

52. C: If the ratio of the corresponding linear dimensions of two similar figures is *a/b*, then the ratio of their volumes is $(a/b)^3$. In other words, if their lengths (or widths or heights) are multiplied by *n*, then their volumes are multiplied by n^3. Since the model and actual building are similar and we are given both of their heights, we should start by calculating the ratio of the height of the actual building to the height of model.

The model is 6 inches tall, which is the same as half of a foot. Therefore, the ratio is 30/(1/2), or 60/1. Cube this ratio, and then multiply the result by the volume of the model, which is 5 cubic feet.
$V = (60/1)^3(5) = 216,000(5) = 1,080,000 \text{ ft}^3$

Secret Key #1 - Time is Your Greatest Enemy

Pace Yourself

Wear a watch. At the beginning of the test, check the time (or start a chronometer on your watch to count the minutes), and check the time after every few questions to make sure you are "on schedule."

If you are forced to speed up, do it efficiently. Usually one or more answer choices can be eliminated without too much difficulty. Above all, don't panic. Don't speed up and just begin guessing at random choices. By pacing yourself, and continually monitoring your progress against your watch, you will always know exactly how far ahead or behind you are with your available time. If you find that you are one minute behind on the test, don't skip one question without spending any time on it, just to catch back up. Take 15 fewer seconds on the next four questions, and after four questions you'll have caught back up. Once you catch back up, you can continue working each problem at your normal pace.

Furthermore, don't dwell on the problems that you were rushed on. If a problem was taking up too much time and you made a hurried guess, it must be difficult. The difficult questions are the ones you are most likely to miss anyway, so it isn't a big loss. It is better to end with more time than you need than to run out of time.

Lastly, sometimes it is beneficial to slow down if you are constantly getting ahead of time. You are always more likely to catch a careless mistake by working more slowly than quickly, and among very high-scoring test takers (those who are likely to have lots of time left over), careless errors affect the score more than mastery of material.

Secret Key #2 - Guessing is not Guesswork

You probably know that guessing is a good idea. Unlike other standardized tests, there is no penalty for getting a wrong answer. Even if you have no idea about a question, you still have a 20-25% chance of getting it right.

Most test takers do not understand the impact that proper guessing can have on their score. Unless you score extremely high, guessing will significantly contribute to your final score.

Monkeys Take the Test

What most test takers don't realize is that to insure that 20-25% chance, you have to guess randomly. If you put 20 monkeys in a room to take this test, assuming they answered once per question and behaved themselves, on average they would get 20-25% of the questions correct. Put 20 test takers in the room, and the average will be much lower among guessed questions. Why?

    1. The test writers intentionally write deceptive answer choices that "look" right. A test

taker has no idea about a question, so he picks the "best looking" answer, which is often wrong. The monkey has no idea what looks good and what doesn't, so it will consistently be right about 20-25% of the time.

2. Test takers will eliminate answer choices from the guessing pool based on a hunch or intuition. Simple but correct answers often get excluded, leaving a 0% chance of being correct. The monkey has no clue, and often gets lucky with the best choice.

This is why the process of elimination endorsed by most test courses is flawed and detrimental to your performance. Test takers don't guess; they make an ignorant stab in the dark that is usually worse than random.

$5 Challenge

Let me introduce one of the most valuable ideas of this course—the $5 challenge:

You only mark your "best guess" if you are willing to bet $5 on it.
You only eliminate choices from guessing if you are willing to bet $5 on it.

Why $5? Five dollars is an amount of money that is small yet not insignificant, and can really add up fast (20 questions could cost you $100). Likewise, each answer choice on one question of the test will have a small impact on your overall score, but it can really add up to a lot of points in the end.

The process of elimination IS valuable. The following shows your chance of guessing it right:

If you eliminate wrong answer choices until only this many remain:	Chance of getting it correct:
1	100%
2	50%
3	33%

However, if you accidentally eliminate the right answer or go on a hunch for an incorrect answer, your chances drop dramatically—to 0%. By guessing among all the answer choices, you are GUARANTEED to have a shot at the right answer.

That's why the $5 test is so valuable. If you give up the advantage and safety of a pure guess, it had better be worth the risk.

What we still haven't covered is how to be sure that whatever guess you make is truly random. Here's the easiest way:

Always pick the first answer choice among those remaining.

Such a technique means that you have decided, **before you see a single test question**, exactly how you are going to guess, and since the order of choices tells you nothing about which one is correct, this guessing technique is perfectly random.

This section is not meant to scare you away from making educated guesses or eliminating choices; you just need to define when a choice is worth eliminating. The $5 test, along with a pre-defined random guessing strategy, is the best way to make sure you reap all of the benefits of guessing.

Secret Key #3 - Practice Smarter, Not Harder

Many test takers delay the test preparation process because they dread the awful amounts of practice time they think necessary to succeed on the test. We have refined an effective method that will take you only a fraction of the time.

There are a number of "obstacles" in the path to success. Among these are answering questions, finishing in time, and mastering test-taking strategies. All must be executed on the day of the test at peak performance, or your score will suffer. The test is a mental marathon that has a large impact on your future.

Just like a marathon runner, it is important to work your way up to the full challenge. So first you just worry about questions, and then time, and finally strategy:

Success Strategy

1. Find a good source for practice tests.
2. If you are willing to make a larger time investment, consider using more than one study guide. Often the different approaches of multiple authors will help you "get" difficult concepts.
3. Take a practice test with no time constraints, with all study helps, "open book." Take your time with questions and focus on applying strategies.
4. Take a practice test with time constraints, with all guides, "open book."
5. Take a final practice test without open material and with time limits.

If you have time to take more practice tests, just repeat step 5. By gradually exposing yourself to the full rigors of the test environment, you will condition your mind to the stress of test day and maximize your success.

Secret Key #4 - Prepare, Don't Procrastinate

Let me state an obvious fact: if you take the test three times, you will probably get three different scores. This is due to the way you feel on test day, the level of preparedness you have, and the version of the test you see. Despite the test writers' claims to the contrary, some versions of the test WILL be easier for you than others.

Since your future depends so much on your score, you should maximize your chances of success. In order to maximize the likelihood of success, you've got to prepare in advance. This means taking practice tests and spending time learning the information and test taking strategies you will need to succeed.

Never go take the actual test as a "practice" test, expecting that you can just take it again if you need to. Take all the practice tests you can on your own, but when you go to take the official test, be prepared, be focused, and do your best the first time!

Secret Key #5 - Test Yourself

Everyone knows that time is money. There is no need to spend too much of your time or too little of your time preparing for the test. You should only spend as much of your precious time preparing as is necessary for you to get the score you need.

Once you have taken a practice test under real conditions of time constraints, then you will know if you are ready for the test or not.

If you have scored extremely high the first time that you take the practice test, then there is not much point in spending countless hours studying. You are already there.

Benchmark your abilities by retaking practice tests and seeing how much you have improved. Once you consistently score high enough to guarantee success, then you are ready.

If you have scored well below where you need, then knuckle down and begin studying in earnest. Check your improvement regularly through the use of practice tests under real conditions. Above all, don't worry, panic, or give up. The key is perseverance!

Then, when you go to take the test, remain confident and remember how well you did on the practice tests. If you can score high enough on a practice test, then you can do the same on the real thing.

Success Strategies

The most important thing you can do is to ignore your fears and jump into the test immediately. Do not be overwhelmed by any strange-sounding terms. You have to jump into the test like jumping into a pool—all at once is the easiest way.

Make Predictions

As you read and understand the question, try to guess what the answer will be. Remember that several of the answer choices are wrong, and once you begin reading them, your mind will immediately become cluttered with answer choices designed to throw you off. Your mind is typically the most focused immediately after you have read the question and digested its contents. If you can, try to predict what the correct answer will be. You may be surprised at what you can predict.

Quickly scan the choices and see if your prediction is in the listed answer choices. If it is, then you can be quite confident that you have the right answer. It still won't hurt to check the other answer choices, but most of the time, you've got it!

Answer the Question

It may seem obvious to only pick answer choices that answer the question, but the test writers can create some excellent answer choices that are wrong. Don't pick an answer just because it sounds right, or you believe it to be true. It MUST answer the question. Once you've made your selection, always go back and check it against the question and make sure that you didn't misread the question and that the answer choice does answer the question posed.

Benchmark

After you read the first answer choice, decide if you think it sounds correct or not. If it doesn't, move on to the next answer choice. If it does, mentally mark that answer choice. This doesn't mean that you've definitely selected it as your answer choice, it just means that it's the best you've seen thus far. Go ahead and read the next choice. If the next choice is worse than the one you've already selected, keep going to the next answer choice. If the next choice is better than the choice you've already selected, mentally mark the new answer choice as your best guess.

The first answer choice that you select becomes your standard. Every other answer choice must be benchmarked against that standard. That choice is correct until proven otherwise by another answer choice beating it out. Once you've decided that no other answer choice seems as good, do one final check to ensure that your answer choice answers the question posed.

Valid Information

Don't discount any of the information provided in the question. Every piece of information may be necessary to determine the correct answer. None of the information in the question is there to throw you off (while the answer choices will certainly have information to throw you off). If two seemingly unrelated topics are discussed, don't ignore either. You can be confident there is a relationship, or it wouldn't be included in the question, and you are probably going to have to determine what is that relationship to find the answer.

Avoid "Fact Traps"

Don't get distracted by a choice that is factually true. Your search is for the answer that answers the question. Stay focused and don't fall for an answer that is true but irrelevant. Always go back to the question and make sure you're choosing an answer that actually answers the question and is not just a true statement. An answer can be factually correct, but it MUST answer the question asked. Additionally, two answers can both be seemingly correct, so be sure to read all of the answer choices, and make sure that you get the one that BEST answers the question.

Milk the Question

Some of the questions may throw you completely off. They might deal with a subject you have not been exposed to, or one that you haven't reviewed in years. While your lack of knowledge about the subject will be a hindrance, the question itself can give you many clues that will help you find the correct answer. Read the question carefully and look for clues. Watch particularly for adjectives and nouns describing difficult terms or words that you don't recognize. Regardless of whether you completely understand a word or not, replacing it with a synonym, either provided or one you more familiar with, may help you to understand what the questions are asking. Rather than wracking your mind about specific detailed information concerning a difficult term or word, try to use mental substitutes that are easier to understand.

The Trap of Familiarity

Don't just choose a word because you recognize it. On difficult questions, you may not recognize a number of words in the answer choices. The test writers don't put "make-believe" words on the test, so don't think that just because you only recognize all the words in one answer choice that that answer choice must be correct. If you only recognize words in one answer choice, then focus on that one. Is it correct? Try your best to determine if it is correct. If it is, that's great. If not, eliminate it. Each word and answer choice you eliminate increases your chances of getting the question correct, even if you then have to guess among the unfamiliar choices.

Eliminate Answers

Eliminate choices as soon as you realize they are wrong. But be careful! Make sure you consider all of the possible answer choices. Just because one appears right, doesn't mean that the next one won't be even better! The test writers will usually put more than one good answer choice for every question, so read all of them. Don't worry if you are stuck between two that seem right. By getting down to just two remaining possible choices, your odds are now 50/50. Rather than wasting too much time, play the odds. You are guessing, but guessing wisely because you've been able to knock out some of the answer choices that you know are wrong. If you are eliminating choices and realize that the last answer choice you are left with is also obviously wrong, don't panic. Start over and consider each choice again. There may easily be something that you missed the first time and will realize on the second pass.

Tough Questions

If you are stumped on a problem or it appears too hard or too difficult, don't waste time. Move on! Remember though, if you can quickly check for obviously incorrect answer choices, your chances of guessing correctly are greatly improved. Before you completely give up, at least try to knock out a couple of possible answers. Eliminate what you can and then guess at the remaining answer choices before moving on.

Brainstorm

If you get stuck on a difficult question, spend a few seconds quickly brainstorming. Run through the complete list of possible answer choices. Look at each choice and ask yourself, "Could this answer the question satisfactorily?" Go through each answer choice and consider it independently of the others. By systematically going through all possibilities, you may find something that you would otherwise overlook. Remember though that when you get stuck, it's important to try to keep moving.

Read Carefully

Understand the problem. Read the question and answer choices carefully. Don't miss the question because you misread the terms. You have plenty of time to read each question thoroughly and make sure you understand what is being asked. Yet a happy medium must be attained, so don't waste too much time. You must read carefully, but efficiently.

Face Value

When in doubt, use common sense. Always accept the situation in the problem at face value. Don't read too much into it. These problems will not require you to make huge leaps of logic. The test writers aren't trying to throw you off with a cheap trick. If you have to go beyond creativity and make a leap of logic in order to have an answer choice answer the question, then you should look at the other answer choices. Don't overcomplicate the problem by creating theoretical relationships or explanations that will warp time or space. These are normal problems rooted in reality. It's just that the applicable relationship or explanation may not be readily apparent and you have to figure things out. Use your common sense to interpret anything that isn't clear.

Prefixes

If you're having trouble with a word in the question or answer choices, try dissecting it. Take advantage of every clue that the word might include. Prefixes and suffixes can be a huge help. Usually they allow you to determine a basic meaning. Pre- means before, post- means after, pro - is positive, de- is negative. From these prefixes and suffixes, you can get an idea of the general meaning of the word and try to put it into context. Beware though of any traps. Just because con- is the opposite of pro-, doesn't necessarily mean congress is the opposite of progress!

Hedge Phrases

Watch out for critical hedge phrases, led off with words such as "likely," "may," "can," "sometimes," "often," "almost," "mostly," "usually," "generally," "rarely," and "sometimes." Question writers insert these hedge phrases to cover every possibility. Often an answer choice will be wrong simply because it leaves no room for exception. Unless the situation calls for them, avoid answer choices that have definitive words like "exactly," and "always."

Switchback Words

Stay alert for "switchbacks." These are the words and phrases frequently used to alert you to shifts in thought. The most common switchback word is "but." Others include "although," "however," "nevertheless," "on the other hand," "even though," "while," "in spite of," "despite," and "regardless of."

New Information

Correct answer choices will rarely have completely new information included. Answer choices typically are straightforward reflections of the material asked about and will directly relate to the question. If a new piece of information is included in an answer choice that doesn't even seem to relate to the topic being asked about, then that answer choice is likely incorrect. All of the information needed to answer the question is usually provided for you in the question. You should not have to make guesses that are unsupported or choose answer choices that require unknown information that cannot be reasoned from what is given.

Time Management

On technical questions, don't get lost on the technical terms. Don't spend too much time on any one question. If you don't know what a term means, then odds are you aren't going to get much further since you don't have a dictionary. You should be able to immediately recognize whether or not you know a term. If you don't, work with the other clues that you have—the other answer choices and terms provided—but don't waste too much time trying to figure out a difficult term that you don't know.

Contextual Clues

Look for contextual clues. An answer can be right but not the correct answer. The contextual clues will help you find the answer that is most right and is correct. Understand the context in which a phrase or statement is made. This will help you make important distinctions.

Don't Panic

Panicking will not answer any questions for you; therefore, it isn't helpful. When you first see the question, if your mind goes blank, take a deep breath. Force yourself to mechanically go through the steps of solving the problem using the strategies you've learned.

Pace Yourself

Don't get clock fever. It's easy to be overwhelmed when you're looking at a page full of questions, your mind is full of random thoughts and feeling confused, and the clock is ticking down faster than you would like. Calm down and maintain the pace that you have set for yourself. As long as you are on track by monitoring your pace, you are guaranteed to have enough time for yourself. When you get to the last few minutes of the test, it may seem like you won't have enough time left, but if you only have as many questions as you should have left at that point, then you're right on track!

Answer Selection

The best way to pick an answer choice is to eliminate all of those that are wrong, until only one is left and confirm that is the correct answer. Sometimes though, an answer choice may immediately look right. Be careful! Take a second to make sure that the other choices are not equally obvious. Don't make a hasty mistake. There are only two times that you should stop before checking other answers. First is when you are positive that the answer choice you have selected is correct. Second is when time is almost out and you have to make a quick guess!

Check Your Work

Since you will probably not know every term listed and the answer to every question, it is important that you get credit for the ones that you do know. Don't miss any questions through careless mistakes. If at all possible, try to take a second to look back over your answer selection and make sure you've selected the correct answer choice and haven't made a costly careless mistake (such as marking an answer choice that you didn't mean to mark). The time it takes for this quick double check should more than pay for itself in caught mistakes.

Beware of Directly Quoted Answers

Sometimes an answer choice will repeat word for word a portion of the question or reference section. However, beware of such exact duplication. It may be a trap! More than likely, the correct choice will paraphrase or summarize a point, rather than being exactly the same wording.

Slang

Scientific sounding answers are better than slang ones. An answer choice that begins "To compare the outcomes…" is much more likely to be correct than one that begins "Because some people insisted…"

Extreme Statements

Avoid wild answers that throw out highly controversial ideas that are proclaimed as established fact. An answer choice that states the "process should used in certain situations, if…" is much more likely to be correct than one that states the "process should be discontinued completely." The first is a calm rational statement and doesn't even make a definitive, uncompromising stance, using a hedge word "if" to provide wiggle room, whereas the second choice is a radical idea and far more extreme.

Answer Choice Families

When you have two or more answer choices that are direct opposites or parallels, one of them is usually the correct answer. For instance, if one answer choice states "x increases" and another answer choice states "x decreases" or "y increases," then those two or three answer choices are very similar in construction and fall into the same family of answer choices. A family of answer choices consists of two or three answer choices, very similar in construction, but often with directly opposite meanings. Usually the correct answer choice will be in that family of answer choices. The "odd man out" or answer choice that doesn't seem to fit the parallel construction of the other answer choices is more likely to be incorrect.

Special Report: How to Overcome Test Anxiety

The very nature of tests caters to some level of anxiety, nervousness, or tension, just as we feel for any important event that occurs in our lives. A little bit of anxiety or nervousness can be a good thing. It helps us with motivation, and makes achievement just that much sweeter. However, too much anxiety can be a problem, especially if it hinders our ability to function and perform.

"Test anxiety," is the term that refers to the emotional reactions that some test-takers experience when faced with a test or exam. Having a fear of testing and exams is based upon a rational fear, since the test-taker's performance can shape the course of an academic career. Nevertheless, experiencing excessive fear of examinations will only interfere with the test-taker's ability to perform and chance to be successful.

There are a large variety of causes that can contribute to the development and sensation of test anxiety. These include, but are not limited to, lack of preparation and worrying about issues surrounding the test.

Lack of Preparation

Lack of preparation can be identified by the following behaviors or situations:

Not scheduling enough time to study, and therefore cramming the night before the test or exam
Managing time poorly, to create the sensation that there is not enough time to do everything
Failing to organize the text information in advance, so that the study material consists of the entire text and not simply the pertinent information
Poor overall studying habits

Worrying, on the other hand, can be related to both the test taker, or many other factors around him/her that will be affected by the results of the test. These include worrying about:

Previous performances on similar exams, or exams in general
How friends and other students are achieving
The negative consequences that will result from a poor grade or failure

There are three primary elements to test anxiety. Physical components, which involve the same typical bodily reactions as those to acute anxiety (to be discussed below). Emotional factors have to do with fear or panic. Mental or cognitive issues concerning attention spans and memory abilities.

Physical Signals

There are many different symptoms of test anxiety, and these are not limited to mental and emotional strain. Frequently there are a range of physical signals that will let a test taker know that he/she is suffering from test anxiety. These bodily changes can include the following:

Perspiring
Sweaty palms
Wet, trembling hands
Nausea
Dry mouth
A knot in the stomach
Headache
Faintness
Muscle tension
Aching shoulders, back and neck
Rapid heart beat
Feeling too hot/cold

To recognize the sensation of test anxiety, a test-taker should monitor him/herself for the following sensations:

The physical distress symptoms as listed above
Emotional sensitivity, expressing emotional feelings such as the need to cry or laugh too much, or a sensation of anger or helplessness
A decreased ability to think, causing the test-taker to blank out or have racing thoughts that are hard to organize or control.

Though most students will feel some level of anxiety when faced with a test or exam, the majority can cope with that anxiety and maintain it at a manageable level. However, those who cannot are faced with a very real and very serious condition, which can and should be controlled for the immeasurable benefit of this sufferer.

Naturally, these sensations lead to negative results for the testing experience. The most common effects of test anxiety have to do with nervousness and mental blocking.

Nervousness

Nervousness can appear in several different levels:

The test-taker's difficulty, or even inability to read and understand the questions on the test
The difficulty or inability to organize thoughts to a coherent form
The difficulty or inability to recall key words and concepts relating to the testing questions (especially essays)
The receipt of poor grades on a test, though the test material was well known by the test taker

Conversely, a person may also experience mental blocking, which involves:

Blanking out on test questions
Only remembering the correct answers to the questions when the test has already finished.

Fortunately for test anxiety sufferers, beating these feelings, to a large degree, has to do with proper preparation. When a test taker has a feeling of preparedness, then anxiety will be dramatically lessened.

The first step to resolving anxiety issues is to distinguish which of the two types of anxiety are being suffered. If the anxiety is a direct result of a lack of preparation, this should be considered a normal reaction, and the anxiety level (as opposed to the test results) shouldn't be anything to worry about. However, if, when adequately prepared, the test-taker still panics, blanks out, or seems to overreact, this is not a fully rational reaction. While this can be considered normal too, there are many ways to combat and overcome these effects.

Remember that anxiety cannot be entirely eliminated, however, there are ways to minimize it, to make the anxiety easier to manage. Preparation is one of the best ways to minimize test anxiety. Therefore the following techniques are wise in order to best fight off any anxiety that may want to build.

To begin with, try to avoid cramming before a test, whenever it is possible. By trying to memorize an entire term's worth of information in one day, you'll be shocking your system, and not giving yourself a very good chance to absorb the information. This is an easy path to anxiety, so for those who suffer from test anxiety, cramming should not even be considered an option.

Instead of cramming, work throughout the semester to combine all of the material which is presented throughout the semester, and work on it gradually as the course goes by, making sure to master the main concepts first, leaving minor details for a week or so before the test.

To study for the upcoming exam, be sure to pose questions that may be on the examination, to gauge the ability to answer them by integrating the ideas from your texts, notes and lectures, as well as any supplementary readings.

If it is truly impossible to cover all of the information that was covered in that particular term, concentrate on the most important portions, that can be covered very well. Learn these concepts as best as possible, so that when the test comes, a goal can be made to use these concepts as presentations of your knowledge.

In addition to study habits, changes in attitude are critical to beating a struggle with test anxiety. In fact, an improvement of the perspective over the entire test-taking experience can actually help a test taker to enjoy studying and therefore improve the overall experience. Be certain not to overemphasize the significance of the grade - know that the result of the test is neither a reflection of self worth, nor is it a measure of intelligence; one grade will not predict a person's future success.

To improve an overall testing outlook, the following steps should be tried:

Keeping in mind that the most reasonable expectation for taking a test is to expect to try to demonstrate as much of what you know as you possibly can.
Reminding ourselves that a test is only one test; this is not the only one, and there will be others.
The thought of thinking of oneself in an irrational, all-or-nothing term should be avoided at all costs.
A reward should be designated for after the test, so there's something to look forward to. Whether it be going to a movie, going out to eat, or simply visiting friends, schedule it in advance, and do it no matter what result is expected on the exam.

Test-takers should also keep in mind that the basics are some of the most important things, even beyond anti-anxiety techniques and studying. Never neglect the basic social, emotional and biological needs, in order to try to absorb information. In order to best achieve, these three factors must be held as just as important as the studying itself.

Study Steps

Remember the following important steps for studying:

Maintain healthy nutrition and exercise habits. Continue both your recreational activities and social pass times. These both contribute to your physical and emotional well being.
Be certain to get a good amount of sleep, especially the night before the test, because when you're overtired you are not able to perform to the best of your best ability.
Keep the studying pace to a moderate level by taking breaks when they are needed, and varying the work whenever possible, to keep the mind fresh instead of getting bored. When enough studying has been done that all the material that can be learned has been learned, and the test taker is prepared for the test, stop studying and do something relaxing such as listening to music, watching a movie, or taking a warm bubble bath.

There are also many other techniques to minimize the uneasiness or apprehension that is experienced along with test anxiety before, during, or even after the examination. In fact, there are a great deal of things that can be done to stop anxiety from interfering with lifestyle and performance. Again, remember that anxiety will not be eliminated entirely, and it shouldn't be. Otherwise that "up" feeling for exams would not exist, and most of us depend on that sensation to perform better than usual. However, this anxiety has to be at a level that is manageable.

Of course, as we have just discussed, being prepared for the exam is half the battle right away. Attending all classes, finding out what knowledge will be expected on the exam, and knowing the exam schedules are easy steps to lowering anxiety. Keeping up with work will remove the need to cram, and efficient study habits will eliminate wasted time. Studying should be done in an ideal location for concentration, so that it is simple to become interested in the material and give it complete attention. A method such as SQ3R (Survey, Question, Read, Recite, Review) is a wonderful key to follow to make sure that the study habits are as effective as possible, especially in the case of learning from a textbook. Flashcards are great techniques for memorization. Learning to take good notes will mean that notes will be full of useful information, so that less sifting will need to be done to seek out what is pertinent for studying. Reviewing notes after class and then again on occasion will keep the information fresh in the mind. From notes that have been taken summary sheets and outlines can be made for simpler reviewing.

A study group can also be a very motivational and helpful place to study, as there will be a sharing of ideas, all of the minds can work together, to make sure that everyone understands, and the studying will be made more interesting because it will be a social occasion.

Basically, though, as long as the test-taker remains organized and self confident, with efficient study habits, less time will need to be spent studying, and higher grades will be achieved.

To become self confident, there are many useful steps. The first of these is "self talk." It has been shown through extensive research, that self-talk for students who suffer from test anxiety, should be well monitored, in order to make sure that it contributes to self confidence as opposed to sinking the student. Frequently the self talk of test-anxious students is negative or self-defeating, thinking that everyone else is smarter and faster, that they always mess up, and that if they don't do well, they'll fail the entire course. It is important to decreasing anxiety that awareness is made of self talk. Try writing any negative self thoughts and then disputing them with a positive statement instead. Begin self-encouragement as though it was a friend speaking. Repeat positive statements to help reprogram the mind to believing in successes instead of failures.

Helpful Techniques

Other extremely helpful techniques include:

Self-visualization of doing well and reaching goals
While aiming for an "A" level of understanding, don't try to "overprotect" by setting your expectations lower. This will only convince the mind to stop studying in order to meet the lower expectations.
Don't make comparisons with the results or habits of other students. These are individual factors, and different things work for different people, causing different results.
Strive to become an expert in learning what works well, and what can be done in order to improve. Consider collecting this data in a journal.
Create rewards for after studying instead of doing things before studying that will only turn into avoidance behaviors.
Make a practice of relaxing - by using methods such as progressive relaxation, self-hypnosis, guided imagery, etc - in order to make relaxation an automatic sensation.
Work on creating a state of relaxed concentration so that concentrating will take on the focus of the mind, so that none will be wasted on worrying.
Take good care of the physical self by eating well and getting enough sleep.
Plan in time for exercise and stick to this plan.

Beyond these techniques, there are other methods to be used before, during and after the test that will help the test-taker perform well in addition to overcoming anxiety.

Before the exam comes the academic preparation. This involves establishing a study schedule and beginning at least one week before the actual date of the test. By doing this, the anxiety of not having enough time to study for the test will be automatically eliminated. Moreover, this will make the studying a much more effective experience, ensuring that the learning will be an easier process. This relieves much undue pressure on the test-taker.

Summary sheets, note cards, and flash cards with the main concepts and examples of these main concepts should be prepared in advance of the actual studying time. A topic should never be eliminated from this process. By omitting a topic because it isn't expected to be on the test is only setting up the test-taker for anxiety should it actually appear on the exam. Utilize the course syllabus for laying out the topics that should be studied. Carefully go over the notes that were made in class, paying special attention to any of the issues that the professor took special care to emphasize while lecturing in class. In the textbooks, use the chapter review, or if possible, the chapter tests, to begin your review.

It may even be possible to ask the instructor what information will be covered on the exam, or what the format of the exam will be (for example, multiple choice, essay, free form, true-false). Additionally, see if it is possible to find out how many questions will be on the test. If a review sheet or sample test has been offered by the professor, make good use of it, above anything else, for the preparation for the test. Another great resource for getting to know the examination is reviewing tests from previous semesters. Use these tests to review, and aim to achieve a 100% score on each of the possible topics. With a few exceptions, the goal that you set for yourself is the highest one that you will reach.

Take all of the questions that were assigned as homework, and rework them to any other possible course material. The more problems reworked, the more skill and confidence will form as a result. When forming the solution to a problem, write out each of the steps. Don't simply do head work. By doing as many steps on paper as possible, much clarification and therefore confidence will be formed. Do this with as many homework problems as possible, before checking the answers. By checking the answer after each problem, a reinforcement will exist, that will not be on the exam. Study situations should be as exam-like as possible, to prime the test-taker's system for the experience. By waiting to check the answers at the end, a psychological advantage will be formed, to decrease the stress factor.

Another fantastic reason for not cramming is the avoidance of confusion in concepts, especially when it comes to mathematics. 8-10 hours of study will become one hundred percent more effective if it is spread out over a week or at least several days, instead of doing it all in one sitting. Recognize that the human brain requires time in order to assimilate new material, so frequent breaks and a span of study time over several days will be much more beneficial.

Additionally, don't study right up until the point of the exam. Studying should stop a minimum of one hour before the exam begins. This allows the brain to rest and put things in their proper order. This will also provide the time to become as relaxed as possible when going into the examination room. The test-taker will also have time to eat well and eat sensibly. Know that the brain needs food as much as the rest of the body. With enough food and enough sleep, as well as a relaxed attitude, the body and the mind are primed for success.

Avoid any anxious classmates who are talking about the exam. These students only spread anxiety, and are not worth sharing the anxious sentimentalities.

Before the test also involves creating a positive attitude, so mental preparation should also be a point of concentration. There are many keys to creating a positive attitude. Should fears become rushing in, make a visualization of taking the exam, doing well, and seeing an A written on the paper. Write out a list of affirmations that will bring a feeling of confidence, such as "I am doing well in my English class," "I studied well and know my material," "I enjoy this class." Even if the affirmations aren't believed at first, it sends a positive message to the subconscious which will result in an alteration of the overall belief system, which is the system that creates reality.

If a sensation of panic begins, work with the fear and imagine the very worst! Work through the entire scenario of not passing the test, failing the entire course, and dropping out of school, followed by not getting a job, and pushing a shopping cart through the dark alley where you'll live. This will place things into perspective! Then, practice deep breathing and create a visualization of the opposite situation - achieving an "A" on the exam, passing the entire course, receiving the degree at a graduation ceremony.

On the day of the test, there are many things to be done to ensure the best results, as well as the most calm outlook. The following stages are suggested in order to maximize test-taking potential:

Begin the examination day with a moderate breakfast, and avoid any coffee or beverages with caffeine if the test taker is prone to jitters. Even people who are used to managing caffeine can feel jittery or light-headed when it is taken on a test day.
Attempt to do something that is relaxing before the examination begins. As last minute cramming clouds the mastering of overall concepts, it is better to use this time to create a calming outlook.
Be certain to arrive at the test location well in advance, in order to provide time to select a location that is away from doors, windows and other distractions, as well as giving enough time to relax before the test begins.
Keep away from anxiety generating classmates who will upset the sensation of stability and relaxation that is being attempted before the exam.
Should the waiting period before the exam begins cause anxiety, create a self-distraction by reading a light magazine or something else that is relaxing and simple.

During the exam itself, read the entire exam from beginning to end, and find out how much time should be allotted to each individual problem. Once writing the exam, should more time be taken for a problem, it should be abandoned, in order to begin another problem. If there is time at the end, the unfinished problem can always be returned to and completed.

Read the instructions very carefully - twice - so that unpleasant surprises won't follow during or after the exam has ended.

When writing the exam, pretend that the situation is actually simply the completion of homework within a library, or at home. This will assist in forming a relaxed atmosphere, and will allow the brain extra focus for the complex thinking function.

Begin the exam with all of the questions with which the most confidence is felt. This will build the confidence level regarding the entire exam and will begin a quality momentum. This will also create encouragement for trying the problems where uncertainty resides.

Going with the "gut instinct" is always the way to go when solving a problem. Second guessing should be avoided at all costs. Have confidence in the ability to do well.

For essay questions, create an outline in advance that will keep the mind organized and make certain that all of the points are remembered. For multiple choice, read every answer, even if the correct one has been spotted - a better one may exist.

Continue at a pace that is reasonable and not rushed, in order to be able to work carefully. Provide enough time to go over the answers at the end, to check for small errors that can be corrected.

Should a feeling of panic begin, breathe deeply, and think of the feeling of the body releasing sand through its pores. Visualize a calm, peaceful place, and include all of the sights, sounds and sensations of this image. Continue the deep breathing, and take a few minutes to continue this with closed eyes. When all is well again, return to the test.

If a "blanking" occurs for a certain question, skip it and move on to the next question. There will be time to return to the other question later. Get everything done that can be done, first, to guarantee all the grades that can be compiled, and to build all of the confidence possible. Then return to the weaker questions to build the marks from there.

Remember, one's own reality can be created, so as long as the belief is there, success will follow. And remember: anxiety can happen later, right now, there's an exam to be written!

After the examination is complete, whether there is a feeling for a good grade or a bad grade, don't dwell on the exam, and be certain to follow through on the reward that was promised...and enjoy it! Don't dwell on any mistakes that have been made, as there is nothing that can be done at this point anyway.

Additionally, don't begin to study for the next test right away. Do something relaxing for a while, and let the mind relax and prepare itself to begin absorbing information again.

From the results of the exam - both the grade and the entire experience, be certain to learn from what has gone on. Perfect studying habits and work some more on confidence in order to make the next examination experience even better than the last one.

Learn to avoid places where openings occurred for laziness, procrastination and day dreaming.

Use the time between this exam and the next one to better learn to relax, even learning to relax on cue, so that any anxiety can be controlled during the next exam. Learn how to relax the body. Slouch in your chair if that helps. Tighten and then relax all of the different muscle groups, one group at a time, beginning with the feet and then working all the way up to the neck and face. This will ultimately relax the muscles more than they were to begin with. Learn how to breathe deeply and comfortably, and focus on this breathing going in and out as a relaxing thought. With every exhale, repeat the word "relax."

As common as test anxiety is, it is very possible to overcome it. Make yourself one of the test-takers who overcome this frustrating hindrance.

Additional Bonus Material

Due to our efforts to try to keep this book to a manageable length, we've created a link that will give you access to all of your additional bonus material.

Please visit http://www.mometrix.com/bonus948/gageometry to access the information.